THAT'S WHY I'M A DOCTOR

MARK BULGUTCH

THAT'S WHY I'M A DOCTOR

Physicians Recount Their Most Memorable Moments

 Douglas & McIntyre

Douglas and McIntyre (2013) Ltd.
P.O. Box 219, Madeira Park, BC, VON 2H0
www.douglas-mcintyre.com

Photos courtesy the individual doctors except where otherwise noted
Edited by Betty Keller
Cover and text design by Shed Simas / Onça Design
Printed and bound in Canada

Douglas and McIntyre (2013) Ltd. acknowledges the support of the Canada Council
for the Arts, the Government of Canada, and the Province of British Columbia
through the BC Arts Council.

Library and Archives Canada Cataloguing in Publication

Title: That's why I'm a doctor : physicians recount their most memorable moments /
      Mark Bulgutch.
Names: Bulgutch, Mark, editor.
Description: Edited by Mark Bulgutch.
Identifiers: Canadiana (print) 20190231696 | Canadiana (ebook) 2019023170X |
      ISBN 9781771622523 (softcover) | ISBN 9781771622530 (HTML)
Subjects: LCSH: Physicians—Canada—Anecdotes. | LCSH: Medicine—Canada—
      Anecdotes. | LCGFT: Anecdotes.
Classification: LCC R705 .T43 2020 | DDC 610.971—dc23

As with most things in life, it's easier to write a book when you're happy. And I am. Just about all the time. That's because of the four people closest to me in the world. My wife Rhonda is not a doctor, but she has kept me physically and mentally healthy for almost forty-four years. Her intuition about medical things is uncanny. She knows when I'm sick before I know it.

My first-born daughter is Melissa. She once cried after a visit to the doctor because she *didn't* get a needle. She thought doctors always gave needles, and she was looking forward to it.

My younger daughter Jessica has visited doctors way too often. Stitches here and there. Broken bones here and there. They always patched her up so she could go injure something else.

My granddaughter Reid enjoys playing with the same doctor kit her mother used to play with. She tells me she does not want to grow up to be a doctor, but it's early yet.

There isn't a day that goes by when I don't feel blessed that they are in my life.

Contents

Introduction

The first person who ever laid hands on me, even before my mother, was a doctor. It was Yom Kippur, the most important day on the Jewish calendar. And the doctor was Jewish. So maybe he didn't want to be in the hospital that day, but when my mother went into labour, he got the call and he did what he was supposed to do—he took care of his patient (my mother, not me).

He pulled me into the world, and since it was still before 11:00 a.m., perhaps he went back to the synagogue feeling pretty good about things. I hope so.

Since that day I'm pleased to say my relationship with doctors has been just the way I like it—distant. I had the usual childhood checkups and illnesses looked after by the family doctor (who made house calls), but nothing serious. I still have my tonsils and appendix.

In the summer between high school and university I had a job at a meat packing plant. In the last few days on the job I managed to cut off the tip of a finger working the meat slicer. One of the supervisors at the shop drove me to the hospital—the same hospital where I was born. Once they stopped the bleeding, the plastic surgeon had a look and said to me, "What kind of career are you planning? Do you think you'll need that finger?"

I wasn't sure if he was kidding. But if he was, I wasn't in the mood. I told him I was going to be a journalist, and the injured finger was one of the two I used to hunt and peck when I typed.

"Okay," he said. "Then we'd better fix it up."

And he did.

I've been two-finger typing ever since, through a long and successful career.

I saw several doctors a few years after I finished university. We were trying to figure out why I had pain in my knees. It took a long while before someone diagnosed Crohn's disease. That's a disease of the bowel, which is a bit of a ways from the knees, which is why the diagnosis took so long. Knee pain is what they call an "extraintestinal complication" of Crohn's.

Once we had a name for the problem, I was referred to a gastroenterologist (a specialist in the gastrointestinal tract). I went through a couple of them pretty quickly. I left the first one behind when I moved from Montreal to Toronto. Then the first Toronto specialist didn't do a very sharp job of tracking the diminished level of iron in my blood.

I found that out from my family doctor, Bill Wishinsky. He called me at work one night just before 10 o'clock. (I worked from about 11:00 a.m. to 11:30 p.m. in those days.)

He said, "How are you feeling?"

I said, "I'm feeling just fine. Why wouldn't I?"

He said, "Well, I just got the results of your blood test, and either they're wrong or you're dead." Lots of doctors, it seems, are would-be comedians. He went on, "The iron count is so low. Are you sure you feel fine?"

He was so worried he told me to go the emergency department of a downtown hospital on my way home. He was going to arrange for a blood test there.

I showed up at the hospital around midnight, had a blood test, and it indeed showed that my iron count really was very low (common with Crohn's) and my gastroenterologist had missed it.

My family doctor told me to dump the specialist. So I did.

I've been with my third gastroenterologist for more than thirty years. His name is Fred Saibil. And he's part of why this book exists.

One of the pleasures of Crohn's disease is the need for regular colonoscopies. Pretty much every year, Fred would schedule me for the procedure. I'd drink some vile-tasting liquid to ensure an empty intestine, report to the hospital the next morning, and be wheeled into a room where Fred would smile at me before knocking me out so he could root around in my insides. He'd write a note for me to read when I woke up. It usually said something like, "It looks like a dog chewed your guts." There's that comedic doctor streak again.

Fred prescribed drugs, hoping to make things better. They never did, but I got used to the symptoms and the disease never really stopped me from doing anything I wanted to do, either as a journalist or as a husband and father. But Fred kept booking colonoscopies and reporting how bad things looked. After more than twenty years of this, he persuaded me that it was time to take out the diseased part of the bowel—my first (and only) surgery.

The good news is that now that I'm missing most of my colon, I don't need colonoscopies. But I'm not entirely off the hook. Fred still inspects my insides. It's called a "sigmoidoscopy" or a "flex sig" for those of us in the know. I still drink vile-tasting liquid to get ready, but not as much of it, and there's no pain involved so I can be awake for the procedure.

During my last flex sig, Fred was manoeuvring an instrument up my backside when he said, "So when are you going to write another book?"

I had written one a few years earlier about journalists. Fred had even come to the book launch. I said, "Well, I have this idea for a book on doctors." I explained the premise. "I want doctors to tell me a story about something that happened in their careers that confirmed for them that they were right to become doctors. So I don't want to know why they became a doctor. I want to hear about some experience that left them so satisfied, so rewarded, so pleased that they said to themselves, '*That's* why I'm a doctor.'"

Fred said, "Sounds good."

"My problem," I said, "is that I have to get a lot of doctors to talk to me, and I don't know many doctors."

Fred said, "I know a lot of doctors." Instead of watching me being pushed out to the recovery room, he walked alongside the gurney and in two minutes he agreed to help me find some of the doctors I needed. He kept his promise, and here we are.

A few other people helped me find doctors as well. There was Ken Sherman, a writer and poet who works out at the same YMCA as I do. And to make sure I had doctors outside Toronto, I asked some of my former colleagues at *CBC News* if they knew any good doctors. David Cochrane, Bruce Rainnie, Nancy Waugh, Caroline Butler, Ian Hanomansing and Steve Silva were especially helpful. Even my son-in-law, Allan Spears, got into the act.

I'm grateful to every doctor for agreeing to speak with me and for being so patient when I asked them to turn medical terms into plain English. I could have made this book 10 per cent longer just by listing all their degrees, honours, awards and titles and the places they've worked, but I decided to let their stories tell you all you need to know about their character.

The stories I have collected are big and small. The doctors told me about helping millions and about helping one. They told me stories from early in their careers and from late. They told me stories about just about every part of the body from the brain to the toes and everything in between.

Some stories don't have body parts at all. Instead, they tackle health policy issues. This is a part of medicine that's becoming more and more important, and the stories are both powerfully engrossing and thought provoking. They provide a look at medicine through a lens you may never have peered through.

What ties all these stories together is a sense of caring. I came away from my conversations with these doctors with a profound understanding of how dedicated they are to making life at least a little better for the rest of us. I hope you will be left with the same feelings after you've read what they said.

Run for a Life

Sunit Das

Photo courtesy St. Michael's
Hospital

FOR SOME DOCTORS, EMERGENCIES ARE a fact of their everyday lives. But each emergency is different. And as a doctor tries to resolve a crisis to save a life, rules can't get in the way.

Sunit Das, who is now a neurosurgeon and brain tumour biologist at St. Michael's Hospital in Toronto, broke the rules one wintry day and has no regrets.

I'll preface this by telling you that I struggled for a long while in medical school trying to figure out whether I belonged there. When I was a second-year medical student, I applied for a Rhodes Scholarship and became a semi-finalist. Had I won, I'm pretty sure I would have gone off to study the humanities. But since I stayed with medicine, I planned to become a psychiatrist. It's probably the least medical part of the medical profession. That was my preference. But somehow I wandered into becoming a surgeon. I hadn't expected that at all. I spent a lot of energy trying to run away from medicine.

The story I'm going to tell comes from my year as chief resident in neurosurgical training. This was in Chicago at Northwestern University. When you're the chief resident in neurosurgery, you live your life like a madman because you're in charge of the whole service. I was on call every other day, but I felt pretty seasoned. I felt like there was nothing that could happen that I couldn't take care of. Call it the arrogance of youth.

My wife and I had just had our first child, a girl, about six months earlier. As is the case with most people when they have their children, having our daughter was life-changing for me. I was enamoured of her. We three lived in downtown Chicago in an apartment building about three blocks from the hospital. I had always told myself that nothing could happen in the hospital that would require me to do something so undignified as to have to run there from where I live. In other words, nothing could be so urgent at Northwestern Memorial Hospital that it couldn't wait for me to walk over.

One Saturday during the Christmas season I was on call, which meant that I had a junior resident in the hospital, and I was at home just in case. My wife's parents had come to visit us from Virginia, and she wanted to take them out for lunch. She said, "We'll be just down the street if anything comes up. Just call me and I'll come right home."

My daughter was taking her noon nap, and about five minutes after she fell asleep, the phone rang. It was Stephen Shafizadeh, the fourth-year resident on call at the hospital. He said, "Boss, I'm in the ER. There is an eight-year-old girl here who's had a sledding accident. She ran into a tree and hit her head. She has an epidural hematoma. She needs to go into the operating room, and she can't make it to Children's Hospital. I'm getting things going. Come in."

Northwestern is an adult hospital. Our children's hospital was Children's Memorial. [It's now called the Ann & Robert H. Lurie Children's Hospital of Chicago.] It was just a few minutes north of us and, typically, if a child came to Northwestern, you'd send them to Children's. But Stephen was on the phone saying, "This kid's got to go to the OR right now. She can't get as far as Children's."

If this had come from anyone else I would have said, "No. You do what we're supposed to do. You put the girl in the ambulance and you get her to Children's." But I trusted Stephen because he was spectacular. When he told me she couldn't make it to Children's, I knew what had to happen.

I couldn't leave for the hospital with my baby daughter taking a nap, so I called my wife at the restaurant. She's also a physician, so she could probably hear the urgency in my voice. I said, "I need you to come home right now."

She put her wallet on the table and said to her parents, "I'm sorry. Enjoy lunch. Pay for it with one of my credit cards. I have to go." And she ran toward our apartment building.

I was standing at the door in my scrubs waiting for her. She ran in and I ran out. I broke my rule and ran the three blocks to the hospital.

I hurried into the emergency room where Stephen was with Mom and Dad and this eight-year-old girl. She had become unconscious while I was running to the hospital. It was clear that everyone was scared to death.

I said to the parents, "I'm sorry I can't talk to you right now. We have to get going. I'll talk to you afterward. You follow us."

I went into the trauma bay and saw this child was dying.

An epidural hematoma is a lethal thing. A lot of people have heard of it now because of the actress Natasha Richardson. She had a skiing accident in Quebec, hit her head and died. Hers was a very typical story. She had a severe head injury, a skull fracture, lost consciousness, but then woke up and had what we call a lucid period. She seemed perfectly fine. She wouldn't even agree to see a doctor. And then catastrophe. She became disoriented and her brain died. You have a very narrow window to intercede.

In the trauma bay we had an anesthesiologist who was a fellow, which means he's more than a resident but not a staff doctor. He looked at me and said, "We don't do kids here." Thankfully, the staff doctor on call that day was a guy named Anthony Koht, who was the chair of neuroanesthesia at the hospital and someone I worked with every day. He walked into the room and asked, "What's going on?"

I said, "We have a young kid with an epidural hematoma and we need to do something now."

Tony looked at the fellow, who said, "We don't do kids here."

Without a word, Tony pushed his fellow out of the way and intubated the kid. That is, he inserted a tube through her mouth and then into the airway. You do this so the patient can be placed on a ventilator to help her breathe during anesthesia. Thank god I had Tony there. He said, "Just go. Just go. Just go."

We took her upstairs to the operating room. The parents followed and I told them to wait outside. I made a call to the staff doctor and he, too, said to go ahead.

Any time there's an emergency case, everyone's kind of in a rush in the OR. This time it was compounded by the fact that our patient was an eight-year-old, and we'd never done anything for an eight-year-old at Northwestern. And it wasn't because we didn't feel like it. There are good reasons for an adult hospital not to treat children. There is a sense that there are doctors elsewhere who can do it better than us, doctors who are meant to do it.

One of the things you hear over and over again during your pediatric rotation as a medical student is that children are not just small adults. So now there was a lot of running around as people looked for IV tubes that were small enough to get into a child's vein as compared to an adult vein. When we do surgery, we put the head in what we call "pins," a sort of medieval clamp that we put into the skull to hold the head in place. The pins used for children are different from the ones we use for adults. So there were some real issues treating this child in our hospital.

I shaved this poor little kid's head. With an epidural hematoma there's bleeding that occurs between the skull and the outer membrane covering the brain. The reason this injury is so dangerous is that the blood accumulates very quickly, putting more and more pressure on the temporal lobe of the brain. This causes the pupil of the eye to become fixed and dilated, and that had already started to happen when we were positioning her to operate. She was actively dying.

We did what for us is a very simple procedure—we opened up her head and took out the epidural hematoma. When we finished up, we closed the skin. There was some debate then about whether or not to keep the little girl asleep and have her transported to Children's.

Tony said, "No." He said, "Wake her up. She's fine."

He took the breathing tube out, and the girl looked at me and said, "I'm sorry."

We then walked her parents into the operating room corridor, which is what they did all the time at Children's but we never did with adults. It was clear they understood how close their daughter had come to death. They were both tearful. They rushed to their daughter when they saw her awake on the gurney outside of the OR. I explained what we had done and what was going to happen next.

The mom hugged me, then the dad. The mom said, "Thank you. Thank you." I was so filled with emotion, it's hard for me to remember if there was anything more. Then they were off with the ambulance crew to Children's.

That was a day I learned something about what it means to take responsibility, a day when the staff doctor was not involved. It was my call. If I had said to Stephen, "No, send her to Children's," that's what would've happened. If I had said to Dr. Koht, "Yes, we can probably get her safely to Children's," that's what would've happened. The weight was on me to say, "I know we don't do this with kids, but this is what we've got to do."

I have no doubt that if I had said any of those other things, she would have died.

The resonance of that day is all the greater because of the little romance I had going with my daughter, who was only six months old. In thinking how much she meant to me, it was impossible to accept that we could have a bad outcome for these two parents. And for the longest time I have thought to myself that if I never do anything else in my life, I did this.

Part of the Family

Lisa Del Giudice

A BIG, MODERN CITY CAN SOMETIMES BE a very cold and impersonal place. People go about their business without making deep connections with each other. Your family doctor doesn't have to be your best friend to provide you with top-of-the-line medical care.

Lisa Del Giudice is a bit different. She runs a family practice, not from a small office in a shopping plaza, but from a major city hospital in Toronto. Still at times she has become very close to her patients.

These two stories are both about cancer. The first story happened in my first year or two of practice. One of my patients was a really delightful man—the kind of guy who would come in and make everybody smile, make everybody feel good about themselves. He would leave, and everybody would say, "Wow, that was a breath of fresh air that just came through here. I don't know why I feel really good, but I do." Just the most delightful man. He came in one day after he was newly diagnosed with diabetes. He was upbeat as always. He said, "I'm going to get over this. I'm going to lose weight, and I'm going to do everything I'm supposed to do."

About three months later his wife, who was also my patient, came in and said, "I know you want him to lose weight but it's kind of ridiculous. He's already lost a lot of weight, but I think it's too much. He doesn't even look good anymore."

I said, "Why don't you have him come in and we'll see what he's doing? Maybe he's doing something not quite right. Tell him to come in."

So he came in and we talked about his diabetes. But then just as I was leaving the room, he said, "Oh, by the way, I'm not really swallowing well. I'm kind of choking on my food these days."

I thought, probably a bit of reflux, ordinary heartburn.

I gave him some antacid, but I ordered an x-ray of his digestive tract as well. When I got the results back, it showed a six-centimetre tumour between his esophagus and his stomach. Cancer. Inoperable cancer. I called him and said, "You need to come in. We need to discuss the x-ray results. And bring your wife with you and whoever else you need."

He came in that same afternoon with his wife and son. I could not get the words out to tell them. I sobbed uncontrollably. I had to leave the room two or three times. I did everything they tell you in medical school not to do when you're giving bad news. I finally got it out and told them that it didn't look good, but I was going to send him to all the specialists to see what they could do. He wasn't even sixty years old.

He was devastated. The wife was devastated. The son was devastated as well. That was the first time I had met the son. He was at university at the time and pretty soon he said he couldn't concentrate on school. He asked me to write a letter to the university explaining that he needed a break and should take off the rest of the semester. I did that. The wife came to see me a couple of times as well. It was really hard on her.

About a month or two later he ended up in the hospital, the same hospital where I practise. The wife came down to my clinic, and she said, "He's asking for you. He has something he wants to tell you. So if you could pass by to see him, he would appreciate it." When clinic ended, I went up to his room. He told everybody else to get out and we closed the door. He started to talk. "I can't do this to my family anymore. Tell me what I can do so I can go to sleep tonight and not wake up tomorrow morning."

I was shocked. At the time, medically assisted dying was illegal. A non-starter. I asked him, "Why would you want that?"

He said, "My son needs to go back to school and my wife needs to get on with her life. I'm just a burden on them right now. I just want to take a whole bunch of pills and die and let them get on with their lives."

We had a long conversation. I remember saying to him, "Where do you think your family would rather be? Do you think your son would rather be sitting in a classroom at the university listening to some boring lecture? He has the rest of his life to hear lectures. And your wife? Where does she want to be? I know she's very much involved in the community and volunteers a lot, but do you think she'd rather be anywhere else than with you? Spending every last precious moment that she's got with you?"

I remember saying, "Your son will get back to school. Taking a year off when he's twenty years old is not a big deal in the grand scheme of things. And all your wife's activities are still going to be there later, but now she wants every precious moment she can have with you. She wants to help you with your daily activities. I'm sure she wouldn't want to be anywhere else. Neither of them will have any regrets about being with you at this time. What could possibly be more important?"

Nothing in medical school had prepared me for that conversation, but something else probably had. My brother had passed away when I was eighteen. He had a stroke. There were just six days from the time he had the stroke to the time he passed away, with a couple of surgeries in between, and I remember wanting to savour every moment he was still alive. I wanted to be there. I didn't want to be anywhere else. I wanted to be by his bedside, and I think if I had been anywhere else, I would've had terrible regrets. So what I said to my patient probably came from my own personal experience.

It resonated with him. His wife came in to see me about a week later and she said, "Whatever you said to him has brought about a complete change. He's writing his memoirs and he's got this whole new outlook. He wants to live now. He's called in his entire family. He wants to see everybody. Every friend. Every relative. He wants to chat with everybody and wants everybody to come visit him."

He died about four months later. I saw the family soon after, and I continue to see the family today. I saw his daughter-in-law the other day. I see his grandchild. Being part of their lives through such a difficult time and having those difficult conversations created a bond. I still feel very connected to that family, still very much a part of that family. I feel I'm a family member, like a niece or a daughter.

The second story is about another family I saw early on in my career. The parents were my patients and so were their four children—twin daughters and two younger sons.

The mother of the family was diagnosed with melanoma. She got through that fine, but then one of the daughters, at about twenty years of age, was diagnosed with a very rare cancer. Only about forty people in North America get it every year, so it's extremely rare. The mother searched for people all over the world who were researching this very rare cancer. She got in touch with them, wanting to make sure she was doing everything right, making sure her daughter was getting the best treatment.

The daughter did well for a period of time—two or three years. Then within about two months of each other, the mother was diagnosed with another cancer and the daughter's cancer came back. This was obviously very hard on the entire family. One of the sons really took it hard. He was not coping well. The dad was not managing well either. So I was seeing him through all of that, just trying to be supportive. The mom got through her cancer okay, but the daughter's cancer got worse before it got better, until after a while her condition was stable. Then one day when the mother was with her daughters, she suddenly passed out. She was brought to the hospital, and the daughters came upstairs to my office and said, "Something just happened to Mom. She passed out and she's in Emergency on life support."

I went down and sure enough she was on life support. She'd had a massive brain hemorrhage. The doctors showed me the imaging, and I could see her brain had been pushed down into the spinal cord. There was no way she would have been able to breathe without life support.

The doctor in Emergency told the family, "We can keep her on life support until you decide what to do." So I sat with the family and had a long session with them about pulling life support on Mom. It was a conversation about letting go, and they came to a decision fairly quickly.

When they decided, I stepped out of the room and they pulled her off the life support. She probably passed away fairly quickly. I sat outside in the emergency area nursing station waiting for the family to tell me it was over. Then I went back in and sat through the evening to help them through it. And again I felt as though I was part of the family.

The daughter was still quite unwell, and she passed away about a year and a half later. That was five or six years ago, but to me it still very much feels as though I've lost two family members. I continue to see the dad, the surviving daughter, and one of the sons, who still lives in the city, and it's like seeing family. I feel like I have the skills to have those difficult conversations and be there for them. It's not even tough. I feel like it comes naturally. I actually feel good being there with them.

That's why I'm a doctor. In both cases I was not just treating the patient. I was treating the whole family and being there to support them all through very difficult times. It just felt like I was part of the family and I still feel I'm part of the family.

Changing the Zeitgeist

Laurence Klotz

IF YOU'RE A MAN OF A CERTAIN AGE OR the significant other of that man, you're almost certainly familiar with the letters PSA. And you know that if a doctor sees a blood test that shows you have too much of it, you're about to have a conversation about prostate cancer. But today that conversation is very different from the conversation you would have had not too long ago. It's much easier. In large part that's because of Laurence Klotz, a urologic cancer surgeon at Sunnybrook Hospital in Toronto.

PSA stands for prostate-specific antigen. It's a protein and it's called that because almost all of it is made by prostate cells and no other organ. All prostate cells create PSA, even healthy ones, but much more of it goes into the blood from prostate cancer cells— about ten times more from prostate cancer cells than from benign prostate cells. In the seventies and eighties it was described as a screening test for prostate cancer. You did a blood test to measure the level of PSA. If it was elevated, the patient was said to be at elevated risk for prostate cancer.

The concept was great, but there were two problems with it. The first is that PSA is made by normal prostate cells as well as cancer cells, and particularly people who have large prostates can have elevated levels of PSA. So using the level of the PSA as a cancer screening test can produce a false positive.

The second and bigger problem is that small bits of low-grade prostate cancer develop normally with age. As a man gets older, the likelihood of his having cancer in his prostate goes up, so in any group of sixty-five-year-old men, about two-thirds have some prostate cancer. But the lifetime risk of dying of prostate cancer is only about 3 per cent, so there's a huge disparity between having these little bits of prostate cancer and actually dying of the disease—a twenty- or thirty-fold difference. In the late eighties, however, there was a lot of enthusiasm for doing the PSA as a screening test. If it was elevated, it would lead to a biopsy, and the biopsy often showed these small bits of low-grade cancer. Almost all these men were getting treated aggressively.

Let me just emphasize that I'm a urological surgeon. I've done something like two thousand radical prostatectomies in my career. So it's not like I'm a therapeutic nihilist [that is, having a belief that there's no point in doing surgery]. Surgery is excellent treatment for the right patients—those who have life-threatening cancer. Unfortunately, the treatment for prostate cancer is not like an appendectomy where you have the appendix taken out, then you heal and you're the same as you were before. Radical treatments for prostate cancer have long-term effects on quality of life. It can leave patients with erectile dysfunction and loss of urinary control. Radiation also affects the rectum.

The other thing you have to understand is that the death you may be preventing by surgery or radiation is not a death that would have happened in a year or two. You're preventing a death ten or fifteen years down the road. The average patient who dies of prostate cancer is quite elderly. So the number of life years saved is really quite small.

When PSA screening took off in Canada, there was suddenly a huge number of patients being diagnosed. It was almost an unprecedented dramatic rise—a huge spike. The PSA of these patients was up maybe because they had large prostates or maybe because they had some cancer. They would have a biopsy. Then if they were found to have some low-grade cancer, 95 per cent of them would be treated radically with either surgery or radiation, and they were suffering the side effects of that treatment. As a result, there was increasing concern about over-diagnosis and therefore overtreatment. It was known at the time, or at least thought by many people, that some of these patients had indolent disease—that is, slow growing and non-metastatic. It grows so slowly it doesn't cause any real problems. But no one had worked out a way to manage these patients conservatively, and so all of them were treated aggressively.

I went to lunch one day with two radiology oncologists, Richard Choo and Cyril Danjoux, and we gave ourselves the assignment that by the end of that lunch we would come up with some kind of strategy to reduce overtreatment. So we sat there and literally chewed over ideas.

It was well known that most patients had a PSA that was only mildly elevated. We also knew that most of the patients with advanced prostate cancer had much higher PSA levels. Yet we treated them all the same. So we came up with a simple idea—why not take these guys with low PSA and just watch it? If it goes up rapidly, we will treat them. But if it's stable, we'll do nothing but continue to watch them and repeat the biopsy once in a while to see if there's a change. Really a simple plan. There wasn't a word to describe this approach, so I came up with the term "active surveillance," which has since pretty much caught on all over the world. But it didn't catch on right away.

We received a grant from Prostate Cancer Canada, and we began managing these patients with low-risk prostate cancer conservatively. We tracked their PSA. We repeated the biopsy. And in about a quarter of them—or a third of them over time—we would find worse cancer, and they would be treated. But for the rest we did nothing. We just kept watching. We published our findings in 2002 after we had been at it for about five years. We had 250 patients and no deaths.

That created a firestorm of controversy. As you can imagine, for my colleagues who make a living taking out prostates or radiating prostates, the idea of not treating patients did not go over too well.

And there was also genuine concern that patients would be undertreated and would die, that there would be unnecessary deaths. I took a lot of criticism early on when this concept was being debated, and a lot of people didn't like it. I heard things like, "Dr. Klotz doesn't care if patients die of prostate cancer, which they will if they use his approach." So there was that kind of backstabbing.

In our first publication, we had three or four years of follow-up, but the thing about prostate cancer is that it takes ten to fifteen years to become lethal. It tends to be slow growing when it presents as a localized disease and can be controlled for many years. One of the major criticisms was: "You're reporting too early. You'll see. You're going to follow these patients for another five or ten years, and you're going to see them starting to fall off the cliff. The mortality rate is going to go up dramatically."

But that hasn't happened. The mortality rate that we reported after five years was zero. After ten years we had a few. Now we've had about fourteen hundred patients and maybe fifteen or twenty deaths. Yes, a few patients die of prostate cancer, and of course each one of those is a tragedy. You're never going to have 100 per cent survival. But about fifteen times as many have died of other causes, and about seven hundred have avoided all treatment and the side effects of that treatment. Those dire predictions have not been borne out at all. Prostate cancer patients have not fallen off a cliff and the mortality rate is very low.

At the beginning patients were skeptical, too. You say to a patient, "Your biopsy showed cancer, but you don't need any treatment." And they look at you as if to say, "What kind of a lunatic have I got for a physician?"

The idea of favourable cancer or over-diagnosis of cancer or cancer as a natural part of aging was not really part of the zeitgeist back then. So there was about a ten-year period of intense controversy and debate. Eventually, to my amazement, the world came around to our way of thinking and now active surveillance is considered the treatment of choice for low-risk prostate cancer pretty much all over the world. And let me tell you about when all this really came home to me.

About two or three years ago I was at ASCO, a meeting of the American Society of Clinical Oncology. It's one of the largest medical conferences anywhere with about twenty thousand people attending. It's not a meeting I go to regularly, but I was at this one, and I saw there was a session on over-diagnosis and overtreatment, which obviously appealed to me. So I thought: Okay, that's kind of interesting. I'll go to that.

It turned out to be a session on breast cancer over-diagnosis and overtreatment. So, there I am sitting in the room with about two thousand people, many of them breast cancer specialists.

The truth is that doctors work in silos. I know people all over the world who are in my area of prostate cancer or general urinary oncology, but I don't know people who are in breast cancer at all, and they don't know me. So, I'm sitting there in this room with about two thousand people and I don't know a soul.

They start talking about their concern about overtreatment of breast cancer. And then they start showing *my* data. One slide after another. And they're saying, "These prostate cancer guys have figured this out." I thought: They're using the term "active surveillance" and showing my data. Wow! Not only have I had an influence in my domain, I've actually crossed into others. That's really something!

At the end of this woman's presentation, I went up to the microphone and said, "That was a tremendous talk. I want you to know I am Laurence Klotz, the author of those studies you just showed."

I got a standing ovation from two thousand people, none of whom I knew. They felt that this was such conceptual progress they had to recognize it. In my mind, to get active surveillance accepted for prostate cancer was satisfying, but now I saw I was influencing the management of breast cancer, a disease I've never treated, one that is not my area at all. That was one of the crowning moments of my whole career.

Since then, active surveillance has been more and more widely accepted. In cases of testicular cancer, kidney cancer and many other cancers, conservative management for patients has been promoted. I don't know anyone in medicine who doesn't care whether they are doing the right thing for their patients. So I knew that if we could convince doctors who were operating on patients at the first sign of cancer that it was the wrong thing, that it wasn't in the grey zone anymore, that it's black and white, then they would change their approach. And that's what's happened.

The Gift of Sight

William Dixon

MEDICINE HAS MADE ASTONISHING progress through the years. But when a new procedure arrives, it may take a long while to refine, and early patients may encounter unsatisfactory results. Those who hear about poor outcomes in others may be reluctant to venture into the same territory themselves.

William Dixon is an ophthalmologist in Toronto. He had to overcome initial resistance from a patient to whom he was hoping to give the gift of sight.

They were two sisters. We'll call them Dorothy and Betty. Dorothy was older. Both developed macular corneal dystrophy. It's a rare condition but it's genetic, so it wasn't surprising that both sisters inherited it.

This disease meant that the front of their eyes, the cornea, had gone cloudy. By the time they were in their mid-thirties, they could only see light and dark and maybe their hands when they held them up in front of their faces. They saw the world as if they were looking through frosted glass. They knew there was something out there, and they might see a shadow, but they weren't going to see very much more.

Dorothy had started treatment back in the late forties or maybe the early fifties. At that time, the only place they were doing corneal transplants was New York City, so she went there and had a famous ophthalmologist do her corneal transplant. It was not a pleasant experience. The stitches to keep the transplant in place were pretty gross. I'm sure every time she blinked she felt like she had a bunch of rocks in her eye. And the way they did stitches meant that nothing was watertight, so she would have had to stay in bed for at least two weeks, lying flat and not doing anything. She would have been fed by a nurse. She wouldn't have been able to get up to walk around. She would've had to use a bedpan. The stitches were left in for six weeks to two months—and after all that, the surgery didn't work. So, she came back home and carried on with her life as she had been living it before the operation.

Her sister Betty saw all this and decided, "Well, I'm not having anything done." She was quite happily independent. She was married and had a daughter. When she went blind, she got herself a guide dog, which took her anywhere she needed to go if she was walking. If she had to go farther her husband drove her around. For many years she was a healthy, well-adapted person who was blind.

Then one day she came into Emergency with a sore eye. One of our residents examined her and saw that she had opaque corneas but that one of them had the equivalent of a corneal scratch on it, and that's what was causing her pain. So she treated it, and it healed.

Pretty soon though, Betty started coming in about once a month with pain in her eye. The resident asked her why she hadn't had a corneal transplant, and Betty said, "Oh, my sister had one that didn't work, and I don't want to risk it. I'm quite independent and I can do everything I want."

This went on for several more visits until Betty finally agreed to see me and talk about a transplant. I examined her and could see the surface of her eyes was breaking down. If you've ever scratched your eye, you know it's acutely painful. Here's why: the cells on the surface of your eye are five layers thick. The nerves that supply the feeling to the eye to tell you when something's wrong come up among those cells, and they usually stop about two layers from the top. If you scratch the eye with a fingernail or a piece of paper, you're scratching past the first couple of cell layers to where the nerves are. Every time you blink it hurts. But with macular dystrophy, you don't need a scratch. The top layers of cells just peel off, exposing the nerves and causing pain. That's what was happening to Betty.

I told her, "A transplant might not work, but the outlook is a whole lot better than it was twenty years ago when your sister had hers. We have new techniques. Your sister suffered with stitches back then, but now we use stitches that are half the width of a human hair. You won't be lying in bed. The stitches will be in for a year and they'll be comfortable. You have a reasonable chance of seeing out of the eye."

It wasn't an easy decision. You might say, "She was already blind. It wasn't going to get worse." But it could have gotten worse because at that time she could at least see light and dark. If a transplant didn't work, she wouldn't even have been able to see that. And when you can't tell light from dark, you can't tell if it's day or night, and you don't know if you should be awake or asleep. It's very disorienting. So when a patient says, "I want to keep my light perception," it's no small matter.

Betty thought about it for a while, and finally concluded that she might as well go ahead and have it done. She had a corneal transplant, which is still the only treatment for that particular condition.

Fortunately, it went well. She healed as expected. There was a dramatic difference just looking at her eye. You could see the coloured part of it and the pupil. Looking at it before the surgery, you couldn't see any of that. It was like there was a white cloud in front of her eye.

She got some glasses, and for the first time in twenty-eight years she saw her daughter. I think she could just barely see her when she was born, but she hadn't seen her clearly since then. Here was a person she loved but had never really seen.

We asked Betty if she would mind doing a little promo for the eye bank to encourage people to have their eyes donated after they pass on. She agreed to do that, and in the interview they asked her, "What do you really like about being able to see?"

She almost burst into tears. "The world is so beautiful."

I said, "Wow! That is really good. I'm really glad I'm doing this."

But the story doesn't end there. Two or three years after the surgery she came into my office one day, and I thought she looked kind of different. And she was. She had looked at herself in the mirror, at a face she really hadn't seen in thirty years, and said, "This is awful. I'm all wrinkly." So she went out and had a cosmetic facelift. It was a completely reasonable thing to do.

Then, after about another ten years, Dorothy said, "Maybe I should try again. Maybe a transplant will work for me this time." So, she went ahead and had a transplant, and fortunately for her the second one did work. She had many years with good vision, and became a little more independent because she could now see where she was going.

I was sitting around with friends the other day, and we got to talking about what we'd do if we could start over again. One of them said he'd be an astronaut. Others said they'd be this or that. I said I'd be an ophthalmologist. I really enjoy what I'm doing.

When the Patient Is the Teacher

Karen Devon

WHEN WE THINK OF THE DOCTOR-patient relationship, it's almost always in the context of a sick person looking for help from a learned medical professional. What can the doctor do for the patient? But it can sometimes be the other way around.

Karen Devon is an endocrine and general surgeon at Toronto's Women's College Hospital. She had an unforgettable experience with a patient—an experience that left her deeply affected.

While I was still in medical school, I was trying to decide which specialty to enter. I was drawn to surgery because of some of the technical aspects as well as the artistic aspects. And I like using my hands. But people were discouraging me from being a surgeon because they felt I could use my personal skills in better ways.

Then I encountered a patient who made everything clear.

I was working at the hospital under a surgical oncologist. When a man arrived at his clinic one day, the doctor pulled me aside and said, "Karen, I want you to meet this patient."

That's pretty unusual. Usually you just go down the list and see whoever you see. So, I met the patient—a man in his mid-forties, and a Christian pastor—who'd been dealing with a diagnosis of metastatic cancer for quite some time. After coming through several surgeries, he and the surgeon had connected over their spiritual and religious beliefs. These were different from my own, but their connection was very compelling. So, the surgeon wasn't addressing only the patient's medical issues. It was more profound than that.

We were seeing the patient on this day because there might be one more procedure that could prolong his life slightly and improve his quality of life slightly. But ultimately the man knew that no matter what we did, he had about three to six months to live. He had been told this in late June, so his goal was to make it to Christmas to have one last Christmas with his family.

That's all I knew about him at the time. It wasn't until later that I found out about a sermon he'd delivered to his church after he'd been told that he was dying. I eventually got a copy of what he'd said. He had spoken to his congregation about his cancer and his surgeon, whom he called "gentle" and "compassionate." He said, "If there are tears, I promise you they are not tears of sadness or regret but of joy that fills me to overflowing."

He thanked God for letting him witness the love of his wife and child. "I do not have to deal with corrosive fear, anger, worry or despair. As dreadful as the disease has been, it's not something I regret. In many ways it has been a gift, deepening my relationship with God with all the wonder and joy that experience can bring, in the anticipation of the mystery of what is to come."

I didn't know about any of this at the time. I just knew about a religious man who was going to die in a few months. So we admitted him to the hospital and operated on him. He asked us to play some spiritual music in the operating room and the surgeon said, "Sure, no problem." We did that for him. And he made it through the procedure just fine.

A little later, I was walking around the halls. I was actually trying to get out of the hospital because I had been there all night on call. I wanted to escape before the surgeon came up to do his rounds because, if I didn't get out, I'd be stuck there for another hour or two seeing patients with him and I was already exhausted. As I passed this patient's room, he called out to me to come inside. So of course I went in. He had me sit down beside him on his bed, and he said, "I want to show you something."

I sat down and he pulled out his laptop computer. As he hit the keys, he explained that he had a son who was about nine years old. He had hired a company that did investigative work to take a photo of his son and manipulate it to show what the boy would look like when he became a man. Because, of course, he knew he would not live long enough to see that transformation.

He showed me the picture of his grown-up son with joy. He obviously had sadness, but his message was, "Look how wonderful he is going to be." It was a very positive thing, but I tend to be pretty emotional at any time, and now I was also sleep deprived, so I basically sat there crying the entire time with this patient.

Then he said, "I'd like to give you something."

He handed me a marble and a printout of a story. It said that when he was given six months at most to live, he had ordered a few hundred marbles—beautiful, hand-painted marbles—from Mexico. Then he'd counted out one hundred and eighty-two of them, one for every day left in his life, and put them in a jar.

He reflected on how few marbles there were, and how precious each of them was. And he was giving a marble to anyone who had shown him an act of kindness. He said he wanted to give one to me— to me, a little medical student.

I don't really know what kind of impact I could have had on him, but he definitely had an impact on me. When I left his room, I was a total mess.

He made it through Christmas, and then he passed away.

I still have the marble.

I was very young at the time, but in retrospect I really feel he was on a mission to teach me something or make me believe something. I still don't know exactly what his message was, but it had its desired effect because I've never forgotten him. It was my encounter with him that cemented my desire to become a surgeon. This was just the way I wanted to connect with people. I wasn't somebody who would be very good at helping the walking well. That just wasn't in my personality. I wanted to deal with serious illness and make strong connections.

There are doctors who are more excited by the scientific biomedical pieces of medicine. I obviously use science and medicine every day. Sometimes it's life-saving. Sometimes it's life-altering. Sometimes it's palliative. But for me it's always been the human connections that are most important. I have this idea, this hope, that by entering very personal and usually important parts of someone's life, I can have a meaningful impact.

A Good Doctor

Shel Krakofsky

Photo by Dalia Krakofsky

IT'S GENERALLY ACCEPTED WISDOM THAT over-involvement in the lives of patients is a sure way to practise bad medicine. It's also generally accepted wisdom that a doctor should never treat a relative because it's impossible to be dispassionate about it.

Shel Krakofsky is a retired general practitioner from London, Ontario, who will tell you that both pearls of wisdom are right. But when his son was born with severe impairments, he learned that a doctor walks a fine line.

Our son Noah, our first child, was born with Down syndrome. He was also born with about every imaginable bad anatomical thing you can have. He was born with two holes in his heart, and to make matters worse he had pulmonary hypertension, a combination called Eisenmenger's complex. It's very rare. I don't think there are twenty cases in Canada in a year.

The basic problem is a lack of oxygen. There just wasn't enough oxygen in his blood. That's called "hypoxia" and it leads to cyanosis, which is a fancy word for blueness. Noah's skin, especially around his lips, fingers and toes, would turn blue.

When Noah was born, my wife Dalia and I were told he had five days to live. After the five days were up and Noah was still alive, we went from London, where we were living, to Toronto to see the top cardiologist at the Hospital for Sick Children. He went through this and that, and he said, "The only thing that will save your son is surgery. But the odds of success are less than 20 per cent. The odds of him dying on the table are twice that."

We said, "Forget it. We're not going to do that. We'll take whatever comes. We'll just take care of him and do what we can."

The cardiologist said that was fine. He told us to call him any time, and we went back home.

The next few years weren't easy. Noah had been born visually impaired and was eventually declared legally blind. He was observed with autism, though it was fairly mild: if you tried to shake hands with him, he'd pull his hand back; he wouldn't hug anybody, and he wouldn't let anybody hug him. But emotionally he was as normal as you or me. He smiled and laughed. He made friendships.

From time to time Noah had to return to the hospital for this, that and the other thing, but he was growing and functioning. We loved him and gave him our attention. When he was five years old, we took him back to the Toronto cardiologist. He was surprised to see us, but he was quite frank with us. He said, "I'm amazed, but I don't think it's going to be much longer."

Well, we never took him back there. Noah went to public school and graduated from high school. Always slower than everybody else, of course. He was both intellectually and physically impaired. He would have his blue spells, but he knew that lying down would make him feel a little better. There were hospitalizations, but he functioned. He was okay.

When he was about thirty years old, he got into serious, serious trouble with the pulmonary hypertension, which we knew was incurable. We also knew there wasn't any treatment for it. And we knew that it would probably kill him eventually. In that one year, he had to go to the hospital four or five times, and each time he was basically told to go home to die because there was nothing anybody could do. They could give him oxygen to make him a little stronger, but there was no medication to help him. It was very tough. There was nothing I could do for him, and there was nothing the medical community could do for him.

Then one day at the hospital as they were ready to send us home again, I said, "I have to speak to a doctor who knows about lungs. You're telling me there's no treatment for this and I should go home, but I'm his father. I can't just accept that. There's got to be something."

They said I could talk to the ICU doctor who was on call and maybe he'd be able to help. And maybe because I was a doctor, they allowed me to sleep in the emergency department that night. They gave me a bed. It was very touching. They had pretty well told me to take my kid home to die, but now they were at least willing to let me grasp at one last straw.

So the ICU doctor came around in the morning, and he said, "Well, there's really nothing I can do. But there's a guy at Victoria

Hospital, Sanjay Mehta, who's doing drug trials on pulmonary hypertension. I don't know if he's getting anywhere, but maybe you can get him to help."

We went home, and now Noah needed oxygen twenty-four hours a day just to be alive. I called Dr. Mehta, and told him about Noah, and he said, "Bring him over here. Bring him right away."

So I did.

Dr. Mehta said, "I'm doing a trial on a drug that's showing promise. But your son would have to qualify before he could join the trial."

Drug companies want the people in trials to be the right people, those who can realistically be helped. They don't want what we might call "hopeless" cases because they might not improve, and then the drug might be declared useless. They want patients who aren't so far gone that the drug won't work. To qualify to get into this drug trial, Noah would have to walk 150 metres in six minutes. There was no way he could do that. Then Dalia came up with an idea. She said that if we hooked Noah up to some oxygen and let him use a walker, he might be able to meet the test. But would that kind of assistance be acceptable?

Dr. Mehta looked through all the paperwork, and he said, "It doesn't say anywhere that you can't use oxygen or a walker."

So Noah strapped on the oxygen pack, leaned on the walker, and I held the stopwatch to time him. And he did it. He qualified for the drug trial.

The drug really worked for him. We were able to bring him home from the hospital. He was on oxygen twenty-four hours a day, but he was gasping less often. His fingernails weren't as blue. His lips weren't as blue. And he was home again.

About a year later, he got into trouble again. We took him back to Dr. Mehta, who was conducting a trial on yet another new drug. Noah began taking it, and I knew after two days it was working really well. I hadn't seen him looking so well in a very long time.

A few years later, it happened again. Noah's condition deteriorated and he had to go back to the hospital. After three weeks there it seemed hopeless to everybody, including him. He wouldn't talk. Wouldn't walk. He was blue again. Short of breath. Gasping for air. No energy. No appetite. No activity. No ambition. He was really down, which was unusual for him as he was generally upbeat and positive.

I thought I had to do something to shake things up. We had this little thing between us every time he was released from the hospital: we would go down to the hospital cafeteria and grab a snack—a doughnut and a Coke, a simple celebration to signal that we were on our way home.

Well, this particular time, as a way to lift his spirits, I kept saying to him, "Tomorrow, no matter what's going on, we're going to the cafeteria to get a doughnut and a Coke."

The days were getting longer and drearier. Then one day he seemed to be a little bit stronger. He still had blue fingernails and blue lips. He was very pale, very weak, and couldn't get up even to use the washroom. But I made the decision that today was the day, and I said to him, "Noah, we're not putting this off anymore. Let's go to the cafeteria and get a doughnut and Coke."

I didn't ask anybody's permission. I put him in a wheelchair, hooked up the oxygen, got a portable IV pole and attached that to the wheelchair, and off we went. We walked past the nursing station. Nobody said a word. Nobody asked any questions.

We got to the cafeteria. He was sitting in his wheelchair and I was sitting opposite him. He took one sip of the Coke, and we both realized that this was a nice try, but it wasn't going to work. I was going to have to take him back to his room.

I got up and he signalled me with his head to come closer to him.

So I came down to his level. You have to understand he was very pale. His face was very blue. He took off his breathing mask—and remember he doesn't like touching people or being touched. He leaned right into me, into my face, and he whispered, "You're a good doctor." But what I heard was, "You're a good father."

[*Editor's Note: Noah recovered from that episode and is still living at home. More than forty-six years have passed since his parents were told he would live for only five days.*]

Stormy Weather

Andrew Lynk

DOCTORS GO TO SCHOOL FOR A LONG time to learn as much as they can about the art of healing. They're taught how the human body works and how to recognize what's wrong when things aren't working. Even at the best of times, there's a lot to handle. But a doctor in Canada sometimes has to deal with a predicament for which there is no training. It's called winter.

Andrew Lynk is the chair and chief of pediatrics at Dalhousie University and the IWK Health Centre in Halifax. He recalls two cases that winter turned into life-and-death struggles.

I practised as a pediatrician for twenty-six years in Cape Breton, and in that rural setting I did a little bit of everything. I would go to deliveries for premature babies—that happened many times—and I'd work with teenagers who had cancer, and everything in between. I would see the little ones and the bigger ones and a whole range of problems that I'd been trained to deal with. I could confer with other doctors, but in terms of emergencies with children, I was often on my own.

Let me tell you about a day roughly twenty years ago. There had been a terrible, terrible snowstorm. We had one or two feet of snow, maybe more. There were howling winds, whiteouts, deep drifts.

I was on call at the hospital in Sydney. About eighty kilometres away, near Baddeck, there was a horrible car accident. Two cars going in opposite directions collided. Each car had a set of parents in the front seat, and one twelve-year-old daughter in the back seat.

Tragically, both sets of parents were killed, but both girls survived the crash. They were brought in by ambulance to our emergency room in Sydney. One young girl was stable. She had a lower-back injury with some spinal cord damage, but she didn't have anything considered life-threatening. So we had our specialists look after her.

The second young girl had a broken leg and was bruised in her belly and chest, and it became clear early on that she had very bad internal bleeding. There was also air between her lung and chest wall, which was causing her severe difficulty breathing. I said to her very gently that I was going to have to put some freezing into the side of her chest and insert a plastic tube, which would take some of the air out and make her breathing better. She was very calm and she said, "Okay," and I did exactly that.

We did a CT scan of her belly and it showed that both her liver and spleen were torn and bleeding. At the time we had a very remarkable and fearless general and vascular surgeon, and he took her up to the operating room, fixed up her liver and took out her spleen.

She came back after that to our adult intensive care unit. We didn't have a pediatric ICU in Sydney, and under normal conditions we would have transported her to the children's hospital in Halifax. There she would have a trauma surgeon and a pediatric critical care specialist looking after her in a specialized ICU with all sorts of high-tech equipment. But there was no way in this howling snowstorm that a medical helicopter or a plane could come up and take her to Halifax, about three hundred kilometres away. So she stayed with us.

I poured more blood and fluid into her to keep her blood pressure up, her kidneys working and her breathing steady, and things sort of settled down. I stayed by her bedside, prepared to stay there all night. Suddenly, at about three in the morning, big gushes of blood came out of her chest tube. I suspected there was a torn vessel inside her chest and that a small blood clot had been serving as a patch. It had finally let go and she'd started bleeding tremendously from her chest.

The surgeon came racing back to the hospital. As I said, he was a well-trained guy who could do just about anything. Some general surgeons are reluctant to work on children and also reluctant to try to repair major blood vessels, especially in the chest. You'd get some who would try it but most wouldn't. He took her back up to the OR and opened up her chest. This time he found the bleeding—a major blood vessel. So he fixed that and sent her back to me.

I poured more blood and fluids and medications into her. We'd been working on her from about 6:00 p.m., and now the sun was coming up on the next day. The skies had finally cleared. Pretty soon a helicopter came up and took her to the children's hospital in Halifax.

It was one of those times when I really felt I had saved somebody's life. Between me and the surgeon we had prevented the death of a twelve-year-old girl—no question.

There's a lovely sequel to the story. About eighteen years later, a young mother came into my office with her daughter. I dealt with the daughter's problem and at the end of the visit the mom said, "Doctor Lynk, you looked after me when I was younger after I'd been in a car accident."

I said, "Really?" But her last name meant nothing to me, and over the years I had looked after so many kids who had been in car accidents that I just didn't associate her with any particular case.

But I knew she was now a nurse, so after she left, I called the place she was working and asked someone there what her maiden name was. He told me, and it all came back to me.

This was the twelve-year-old I had looked after on that snowy night almost two decades earlier. It was wonderful to see her doing so well. She was a productive nurse in her community, and she had a family of her own. She was leading a good life—and I felt I had been part of making her story possible.

Cape Breton snowstorms seem to be worst in spring, and my second winter story happened in the month of April. This was another blizzard with howling winds and blinding snow. I was on call at home, and at about six in the morning I got a call from a family doctor at a community hospital in Glace Bay, which is about a half-hour drive from Sydney. He had just delivered a baby that was in very bad shape. Pale white. Blood work awful. Not breathing well. Just shutting down. They didn't have a lot of equipment to help the child. They couldn't even put an IV in to help him breathe, so they were breathing for him by using what we call a "bag valve mask," squeezing air into him by hand. They were holding onto this baby's life by a thread. Our ambulances couldn't go out to get this kid because the snow blocked everything, so our transport team of neonatal nurses with their incubator was of no use. Nothing was moving.

What to do? I remembered my neighbour up the street, Harvey McPhee, who had a big SUV. I called Harvey—woke him up, in fact. "Harvey," I said, "here's the situation." After I explained, I said, "You have a four-wheel-drive vehicle with big tires. Do you think we could try to make it out to Glace Bay? Do you think you can get me there to help this baby?"

He said, "Sure. Let's go." But the snowdrifts were so deep that he added, "I can't take a chance on stopping at your house. I'll just slow down and you're going to have to jump in."

When he got to my place, he leaned over and opened the door, and I jumped in. I closed the door and off we went, plowing through the snow in his four-wheel drive. When we got to the highway, it got a little easier because the wind was blowing so hard it had blown the middle of the road clear. So we drove right down the centre of the highway, with huge snowdrifts on both sides of us. There was nothing else moving on the road so we knew we wouldn't hit any-thing. It took us twice as long as usual to get there, but we made it to the hospital.

The baby looked like death warmed over but I was able to put an IV into him and give him fluids and medicine. I put a tube into the baby's windpipe and started breathing for him, and he began to look a little better. A couple of hours later a snowplow made it to the hospital. We put the baby in an ambulance, and with the plow and a police escort we got the baby back to Sydney.

There's a sequel to this story, too. I saw that child four or five years later. He had some mild impairments, but he was smiling, walking, talking, and doing all the things most four- and five-year-olds should do.

I often wonder about the impact I'm having. When I first saw these two, their lives were right on the edge. But seeing both of those kids later on—one as an adult and one as an older child—it brought home to me that, with my colleagues, I really helped save their lives. It's a great feeling to know that I just happened to be in the right place at the right time to help out. It's very rewarding as a physician. It's why we doctors do this job, even with all the long hours and all the stress. It's pretty cool.

Upstream, Downstream

Ak'ingabe Guyon

Photo by Kinga Michalska

AROUND THE WORLD, UNTOLD BILLIONS of dollars go into medical research every year. No one argues against looking for new treatments, or even cures, for the diseases that plague us. But what if we didn't need new treatments or new cures because the diseases could be prevented? That's the general working premise for doctors of preventive medicine.

Ak'ingabe Guyon is such a doctor. She is a public health and preventive medicine specialist at Santé Montréal, Montreal's public health unit.

I did my undergraduate degree in physiology at McGill University. I was a real keener, enthusiastic to understand how the human body works. Kidneys, lungs, everything. Then I did a master's degree in epidemiology, which is the study of who gets sick or injured and why. By this time I was already realizing that a team of people from multidisciplinary fields could lead people to healthier lives. Health is not necessarily dependent on a single doctor.

After completing my master's, I went to work for a year in Tanzania with a great team of physicians, researchers and colleagues from multiple professions. And it struck me again that, especially in a place with few resources, like Tanzania, the health outcome of the entire population could not be determined only by their limited access to doctors. There was no way we could achieve improved health for everybody if we tried to do it one patient at a time.

Being very convinced of this, I entered medical school. I was going to become a doctor in order to improve health not just individual by individual but at the scale of communities or whole populations. I did my family practice training, further specialized in public health, worked in rural Quebec for a while and then came back to my hometown, Montreal, to work in public health.

There are public health units right across this country. They're called different things in different provinces, but they're all preoccupied with the same things: What keeps people healthy in a community? What makes people sick? What can be done to improve the overall health of the population? These public health units pilot new projects, which they then evaluate for effectiveness and adjust if necessary. And they're on continuous alert for threats to public safety. For example, when SARS [severe acute respiratory syndrome] broke out in Toronto in 2003—more than four hundred cases were reported and forty-three people died—it was public health that coordinated the response.

In 1999 the Centers for Disease Control in the United States issued a report showing that in North America we are living thirty years longer than our grandfathers and grandmothers. But of those thirty years, only five were due to curative care. The other twenty-five years were due to prevention—things like vaccination, tobacco control, work safety and road safety. These are spectacular successes. Of course, I'm not saying this gain in life expectancy is all due to public health units, but public health people have been part of these successes, collecting and studying health data that lead us to where the facts point. This can mean implementing changes through the municipal system, the schooling system, provincial safety laws or the health care system. That's what improves health.

It stands to reason that if you cut the effectiveness of these public health units or diminish their capacity to respond to emergencies, it's not just one person who suffers. It can be hundreds or even thousands of people. But in 2015 a bit of a political thunderstorm hit public health in Quebec: the government decided to cut regional public health teams by a third. That was a huge cut, truly unheard of in Canada. And it made no sense, really no sense. Quebec had been seen as a pioneering province in terms of public health. It had a very solid reputation.

The government was saying these cuts were administrative and they were trying to sell them as a bureaucratic thing—fewer paper pushers, people no one would miss. But they weren't administrative cuts at all. They were going to fire epidemiologists, demographers, nurses and nutritionists, and they were doing it without providing any evidence that it wouldn't hurt the health of the population, let alone improve the situation. Sadly, all this was happening even though the premier and the health minister were both doctors.

It's sobering to realize most doctors work downstream. By this I mean they are doing the very important work of clinical medicine, but this is like catching people once they fall into the river, where they risk drowning. That's what the clinical system does. That's what the health care system does. It's all downstream. But in order to improve health at the whole population level, work has to be done upstream. You have to make sure people aren't falling into the river in the first place. So you have to figure out why they're falling in. For example, if they fell in while cycling or driving, is it because the curve in the road is too sharp? Answering the question of *why* is the work of public health.

Imagine your car is broken and battered, and you don't know why. You bring it into the garage and the mechanic fixes it up. But a few weeks or a few months later you're back. What's going on? What's the real problem? Is it that the roads are unsuitable for driving? Are there too many potholes? Are the lanes poorly marked? Is the lighting bad? Is the signage unclear? Maybe the problem isn't really the car, which is downstream, but the road, which is upstream.

Public health is always about stepping back from an acute situation to see *why* it is happening. As a doctor my job is still to make a diagnosis, propose treatments and follow patients to see if the treatment is working, but the difference between my job and that of most doctors is that I don't work one-on-one but on an entire population. Most doctors—and that includes the doctors who were running the government of Quebec in 2015—see acute situations every day. That's their focus. They put emphasis on the curative system but maybe not on what truly makes a difference in health and survival and quality of care, which is prevention.

Because of the government's decision to cut the public health care budget, one-third of our teams were disappearing from one day to the next, and I could not just stay silent. In my role as a professor at the University of Montreal, I collaborated with a colleague to write an article that was published in the *Canadian Journal of Public Health* in January 2017. For a scientific journal the title was very blunt: "Public Health Systems Under Attack in Canada." Our conclusion was straightforward: "The available evidence suggests that imposing budgetary constraints and dismantling the public health workforce is unfounded and dangerous. Investment in public health has significant and quantifiable impacts in improving population health, with well-documented returns on investments."

Publication gave me a very deep and strong feeling of accomplishment. I felt that this was why I became a public health doctor. Being a physician allowed me to step up, raise my hand and say, "There's something very wrong happening here, and it will certainly harm public health." I have the privilege of being able to raise major concerns when there are political decisions that go against health. Because I'm a doctor I have a trusted voice when it comes to concerns about health, but I am an even more trusted stakeholder because I am a public health practitioner.

When I think about why I am a doctor, I am reminded of the Hippocratic oath, which says we should never intentionally harm our patients. I think that means we also have an obligation to raise our voices when there are measures being proposed that we believe will hurt people. It may not be the conventional way you imagine doctors protecting patients, but it is my way. Prevention is key to the health system and undermining prevention really harms the population in fundamental ways.

Unfortunately, the cuts in Quebec have not been reversed, but there was major news coverage about our concern over them. And when the media pays attention, the population pays attention, so now there's much more awareness of what's at stake. We made the case that reducing the effectiveness of public health units didn't pass any evidence-based test.

Now we have a new government in the province, and during the election campaign they promised to make sure that Quebec was at least on par with the other provinces when it comes to public health resources. Time will tell if they live up to the promise, but we will keep pressing.

For now at least, what we've done is akin to stopping a life-threatening hemorrhage. Stopping further cuts ensures that millions of people over decades will still benefit from prevention and avert a considerable number of avoidable deaths and illness.

No one is denying that downstream medicine is essential. When I'm sick, I want someone who is empathetic and competent to care for me. But there is a place for more than acute-care doctors. There's a place for the work of prevention.

The Path Taken

John Telner

Photo by Betty Telner

SOME OF THE MOST SERIOUS ILLNESSES affecting the human condition are immune to treatments that rely on the steady hand of a surgeon or the latest miracle drug from a research lab. When the mind betrays you, finding a way to cope with day-to-day life is often very difficult.

John Telner of Ottawa is a clinical psychologist who, with others, helped pioneer a treatment for mental illness and has helped patients for several decades. Two cases in particular illustrate the importance of rapport between therapist and patient.

I started off my career in Montreal pursuing a doctorate in physio-logical psychology. (It's now called neuroscience.) It was all brain and behaviour, and I worked exclusively with lab rats. Then I moved to Ottawa to work with two professors in the department of phar-macology at the University of Ottawa's School of Medicine. I started to get into the clinical area by taking clinical training and working on animal models of depression.

When my post-doctoral fellowship was ending there, I was planning to come back to Montreal. But one Friday night I got a call from Dr. Yvon Lapierre, a psychiatrist and psychopharmacologist who had become one of my mentors after I came to Ottawa. He said, "John, it's time for you to come over to the hospital."

A little later my wife, Betty, called me. I explained that Dr. Lapierre had just asked me to start working at the hospital.

And she said, "To do what?"

I said, "Well, to see patients."

"But you don't know anything about patients," she said. "Why would he possibly want you?"

In spite of that, I began specializing in the clinical treatment of depression at the hospital. I was probably only the second person in Ottawa using a new technique called "cognitive behavioural ther-apy" (CBT), which is of course very common today. CBT was invented by Aaron Beck, a psychiatrist at the University of Pennsylvania. He had started out as a psychoanalyst and came to realize that his depressed patients didn't only have problems with mood. They had problems with thinking. Their thinking was off. His idea was that people with disorders such as depression really had, in a sense, a thinking disorder (in addition to other factors). Their thinking didn't cause their depression. But when they became depressed, their thinking processes changed, becoming highly irrational. With CBT we offered patients tools to change their thinking while they were depressed.

There was also a behavioural component to this therapy. Most people who are depressed just want to lie in their beds and do nothing. But we thought if we could get them to the gym every day or have them engage in pleasant activities they would probably see an elevation in mood. We presented them with what might be incorrect in their thinking while they were depressed and gave them techniques to change that. With CBT we don't generally deal with causes. We deal with symptoms. We focus mainly on the present and the future, not the past.

When I started, I was obviously still wet behind the ears. Regardless, I was told, "You're going to run group therapy for depressed inpatients."

I said, "Oh my god." But I scrambled around, got a little more training and went at it. In one of my very first groups, a twenty-one-year-old woman was suffering from schizoaffective disorder (a combination of schizophrenia and a mood disorder, in this case depression). Most people with schizophrenia have hallucinations and delusions, but she had tactile hallucinations. She could feel things that weren't there, like a hand on her back. Plus she had frightening hallucinations, like seeing blood dripping out of her head. They were scary for her and I was scared for her. It was really horrible. She was being treated with medication though not very successfully. She was very intelligent. She already had a bachelor's degree and she wanted to go on to her master's, but she was too ill to do that.

She had been asked to attend my group because of her depression, but she soon became quite angry with me. "You don't understand anything about people," she said. "You just know about techniques. You're not empathic. All you want to do is teach us how to control our depression and our moods."

I admitted to her that I was fairly new at this, but that I was going to try my best to help her. The next thing I knew, she'd made a request to see me individually outside the group. I thought she was still angry with me, and I said to myself, oh boy, it's going to hit the fan now.

But when she came to my office, it turned out there had been some sort of change in her. Although I didn't know much at the time about schizophrenia, I knew a fair amount about depression. I continued to see her for many years. She sticks out in my memory because she was one of my first very difficult patients, but we ended up with an excellent rapport. That proved to be crucial. She had already made several suicide attempts, and she told the nurses, her psychiatrist and me that if she was not "cured" by the age of thirty, she was going to commit suicide. But there is no "cure" for schizophrenia—just adequate control if you're lucky—so around the time of her thirtieth birthday, we persuaded her to check into the hospital so we could keep an eye on her.

If you have good rapport with a suicidal patient, you can sometimes negotiate a no-suicide contract. The deal is that while you are treating them, you will be available to them on an "as-needed" basis, and in exchange they promise not to commit suicide. That's the deal I had with her.

Then one day, as she was doing so well in the hospital, she was given a day pass. She headed for a bridge connecting Ottawa to Gatineau, prepared to jump. But then she thought about our no-suicide pact and, because she was very religious, she didn't jump. She later told the nurses she was angry with me because our pact prevented her from jumping. Her Christian beliefs made her promise to me stronger than her wish to kill herself. She really gave me hell the next time she saw me, but the rapport between us became even stronger.

I continued to see her until she moved away from the city. For many years after that she would send me a Hanukkah card, and the fact that she has stayed alive all these years is very meaningful to me. She said she found the cognitive therapy very helpful, and part of that success was due to the bond between us. I soon learned that if you don't have good rapport with your patient, the CBT techniques won't work nearly as well. I saw this happen over and over as I continued to work with depressed patients.

Later I went to Harvard University to take summer workshops on treating people with obsessive-compulsive disorder (OCD). I learned from the best and afterward I became the go-to person for CBT treatment of OCD patients at my hospital. And I mean extreme OCD. I'm talking about people who were so impaired by their obsessive-compulsive disorder that they couldn't work or leave home. It's a very painful and psychologically debilitating disorder.

People think it's amusing when they're a little picky or overly neat to say, "Oh, I have OCD." But OCD is not a little bit of neurosis. It is a really significant illness that completely destroys lives. The most intelligent people have the most irrational thoughts. I've had people from all walks of life—scientists, doctors, lawyers—who were perfectly rational in the way they did their work, but irrational in their thoughts. It's an illness. It has nothing to do with intelligence. It has everything to do with the illness.

The worst case I had was a man who didn't wash his hair for six years. It was too difficult for him to take showers because it took him hours to prepare the shower. Everything had to be just perfect. He had pathological slowness. He had to wash himself in a very characteristic pattern, and if he didn't do it exactly right, he had to start all over again.

I remember one patient in particular: a fifty-seven-year-old woman, married with two children. She was university-educated though no longer working, and her husband had just retired. She had a terrible fear of getting AIDS, so she would avoid anybody who'd had surgery because they had been in a hospital, and she thought she might get AIDS from them. She avoided the bathroom in her house because a relative who'd had heart surgery had once used it. She would avoid certain shoes because they had been worn in a hospital. She made her husband take off his street clothing when he came home because she worried that they could be contaminated. She wouldn't allow clothes she had worn to touch her clean clothes, so she had different closets for clothes that had never been worn as opposed to those that had been worn once. She avoided hotels, but if she had to use one, she brought her own sheets and towels. She avoided a particular McDonald's because one of the servers there looked as if he could possibly have had AIDS. It went on and on.

Why she became significant to me was that she was my first OCD patient to actually get better. We used a technique called "exposure and response prevention," which is evidence-based and now the standard treatment for OCD outside of medication. We set up a hierarchy of things she found difficult and chose the least difficult thing. We then got her used to it by repetitive exposure, a process called "habituation." We brought in the shoes that petrified her and made her sit beside them. She would become anxious, of course, but her anxiety level would gradually fall. Then maybe she could touch the shoes. Over time we moved up the hierarchy to the next least difficult thing. She was never cured but she got her fears under good control.

It took about a year for her to be able to go to that McDonald's and just sit and look at the young man who appeared to her as though he might have had AIDS. She was never able to make it to the offices of the AIDS Committee of Ottawa. She just said, "I'm not going to do that." It was one step too far for her.

The process is very behavioural and very mechanical, but when I saw it work, I was thrilled. You can read about treatments in textbooks, but when you see them actually working with your patients, you say, "Wow!"

One of the biggest things we get in this profession is gratitude from a patient—a thank you. It doesn't happen often, but when it does, it feels really good. I once got a note from a former patient that said, "I don't know if you remember me, but I had social anxiety disorder. I couldn't even talk to people. Now I'm a lawyer and I got married thanks to your treatment." Another patient sent me a card in the mail thanking me that she was still alive on her sixty-fifth birthday.

I've had a career where I think I did make a difference, and it was much better than the path I was on, working in a lab with rats. Of course, the findings that came out of that lab provided basic advancement, but in clinical work I've actually seen people improving, and that's made me feel very good about the path I chose.

Allergic Reaction

Stephan Malherbe

YOU CAN BE ALLERGIC TO ALMOST anything: peanuts, ragweed, milk, drugs, bee stings, metals, leather, sunlight, even water. Most people with allergies have mild reactions. Sometimes a reaction can be a little worse—call it "unpleasant." Then there are the potentially fatal allergic reactions.

Stephan Malherbe was confronted with one of these. He is now a pediatric anesthesiologist at British Columbia Children's Hospital, but long before he started to work at a major hospital in Canada, he faced a life-and-death situation without the benefit of modern equipment and an army of health professionals.

I did my training in South Africa and, in their system, you go right from high school into medical school. So I was very young when I finished—just twenty-three years old. I worked in rural areas for a couple of years and got a lot of experience in those under-resourced communities.

I came to Canada and worked as a family doctor for a while, but then I went back to South Africa to train as an anesthesiologist. After four years, when I finished my final exam, I went home to visit my parents. I had grown up in a very small village called Barkly East about a thousand kilometres from Cape Town. My father had been a farmer, but by this time he'd given up the farm and he and my mother were living in the little village.

The night I arrived I was just talking to my parents when the phone rang. My father's cousin was still running a farm, and his wife was on the line. She had heard I was in town and she said, "My husband is not well. He's really struggling to breathe. Would you mind coming out and having a look at him?"

As I said, this was my father's cousin, and though I hadn't seen him in a while, I knew him well. When I was a small boy, we were very close. I said, "Of course I don't mind. I'll be right there."

It was probably a five-kilometre drive to the farmhouse. It was raining really hard at the time, but it still didn't take long to get there. It was going through my mind that maybe he was having an allergic reaction. I knew he had an allergy to wool, and he was shearing his sheep at the time. The medical term for his condition is "hypersensitivity alveolitis," an inflammation of the lungs more generally known as "farmer's lung."

It makes no sense, of course, for a man who's allergic to wool to be raising sheep, but that was his livelihood. He had lived on that farm all his life and he loved it. He would try to minimize his exposure to the wool as much as he could by bringing in shearing teams to work on his sheep. But I suppose he would check in from time to time and even that brief exposure could cause a problem. His physician had warned him to stay away.

I walked through the door, took one look at him and could see he was in trouble. He was really, really short of breath. It was a struggle for him, and he was tiring just from the effort of breathing. Sometimes the work of breathing is so hard that you actually use more oxygen in the process than you get into your lungs. He was starting to become a little confused, and he wasn't finishing his sentences. These were very bad signs. Unless I did something, he wasn't going to last long. This man, who was just sixty-three or sixty-four years old, was going to die.

There was no one to turn to for help. There was a physician in town, but he would not have been able to cope with this at all. I had just finished my training and I thought, this is kind of what an anesthesiologist does. I said, "I'm going to take you to the hospital." But when we got there, I saw it was a very rural, under-resourced hospital, and he was getting worse. His lungs were filled with fluid. It was becoming more and more clear that he was not going to make it through the night. He was that sick.

The only way I could help him was to take him into the little operating room in the hospital, sedate him and put a breathing tube down to get air into his lungs. I put the tube in but they didn't have the facilities to keep him breathing. There was no ventilator. I had to manually breathe for him—what we call "bagging." You attach a respirator bag to the breathing tube and then squeeze the bag to deliver air into the patient's lungs. And you keep squeezing in a regular rhythm.

The doctor who lived in the area came in. He was out of his depth, but he managed to phone the hospital in Bloemfontein. That's a city of about half a million people so the hospital there is well equipped.

We agreed that the only way this man was going to survive was if I could get him into the back of an ambulance and "bag" him all the way to Bloemfontein, which was about three and a half hours away.

The local ambulance wasn't equipped for real emergencies. It had a stretcher and that was about it. But we put him in, and then a nurse jumped in to help and we got on the road. I started him on some medication to help his heart along a little, and I just kept squeezing the bag. Squeezing. Squeezing.

After about an hour we stopped at a town called Aliwal North. It had a small hospital where there still wasn't a ventilator, but we picked up a monitor so I could keep a closer eye on his condition. We were still two and a half hours from Bloemfontein. Squeezing. Squeezing. By the time we got there, at 2:00 a.m., it felt like six hours. They were waiting for us and immediately put him on a proper respirator. We got back in the ambulance and arrived back home just as the sun was coming up.

He was on the ventilator for the next four or five days. By then the inflammation in his lungs had settled down and they took the breathing tube out. He survived.

It made me thankful, appreciative and privileged to have undergone the training that saved his life. I was in the right place at the right time. It was incredible. Had I not been there, they would have done what they call a "scoop and run"—they would have put him in the ambulance and made a dash for the big hospital. I don't think he would have survived the trip.

I find being a physician is a calling and a privilege. I feel strongly that we should not take that for granted. One needs to give back to the community. I find physicians sometimes complain too much and think about money too much. But that's not what it's all about.

I enjoy my job most when I'm given responsibility, when I'm challenged and when I have room to grow. Those are the things that make me love my work. On that day I was taking care of a man who was almost like my father, but I had this sense of calmness. This was a scenario I had gone through in my training so many times that I was really comfortable and confident.

To this day my father's cousin remembers the anniversary of that night. When I see him, he says, "It's been five years." ... "It's been six years." ... "It's been ten years." Every year. I managed to save him and pull him through and he's now in his eighties. It was a feel-good moment—a moment that made me really proud to be a doctor.

Shooting Stars

Photo courtesy Collaborative
Family Healthcare Association

Ajantha Jayabarathan

OVER A LONG CAREER, PRACTISING medicine means interacting with literally thousands of patients, and every encounter has the potential to yield a moment of great personal, long-term significance for the doctor.

Ajantha Jayabarathan came to Canada with her family from India when she was a teenager. She is now a family doctor in Halifax, and she has seen literally thousands of patients. But her proudest moment as a doctor happened when there wasn't a patient anywhere in sight, though her patients were top of mind.

I did my medical training in Ontario, but when it came time to do my residency, I wasn't quite certain what kind of doctor I wanted to be. When you are going through medical school, being a specialist is truly glorified. In order to feel that you have somehow accomplished what is essential, and particularly if you value rising to the top and being the best you can be, somehow being a family physician is just not going to cut it. So, at the time ophthalmology was something I thought about. Neurosurgery was also something I thought about. I truly liked these specialties. But I was hyper-focused on my career and the world that medicine introduces you to.

The one thing I did know about the specialty I chose was that I needed to be in a place where I could really get next to patients. I knew that if I went to a big hospital, then as a resident I'd be lucky to be able to touch a patient, let alone manage their care. Fortunately, in Nova Scotia at that time a resident could go to a community-based hospital where there was literally a surgeon, an internist and the resident, in that order of authority. The resident essentially ran the ward. They saw patients in the emergency department. They admitted them. They discharged them. They did it all. So, I chose to come to Nova Scotia.

If a resident had finished medical school but still didn't know what they wanted to become, they could do a rotating internship through internal medicine, surgery, family medicine, all the things they needed to hang up a shingle as a general practitioner. I decided to go with that, and I fell in love with it. I discovered I was a generalist at heart. But I remember walking into the emergency department one day during my residency to do my shift. There was a very old doctor there, and I mean old in a respectful way—a wise senior clinician. After an hour or two he said to me, "Why are you doing this residency for slow learners? You seem too smart for that."

He captured in a nutshell how family doctors are often seen within the profession—as slow learners. I didn't know what to say to him, so I stayed quiet. But over the years I came to realize that general practitioners deal with that perception so often that we come to see ourselves through that lens—if you're told something enough times, you will believe it. But twenty-five years later I honestly believe that being a generalist is one of the hardest things in medicine. I am a proud to say that whether a newborn or a ninety-year-old man or woman comes into my office, I can look after them. I would challenge any of my specialist colleagues to say the same. A cardiologist may tell you the nuances of the electrical conduction of pathways in your heart, but he cannot look after a newborn or a ninety-year-old man or woman. It's taken me a long time to realize that I have value, and I think many of my family medicine colleagues have had trouble over the years seeing themselves as valuable. There's just so much coming at us from the outside world—especially now from government—that devalues us. So that's the background for the story that's to come.

When I was ready to open my practice, it happened to be at a time when the Nova Scotia government had decided there were too many doctors concentrated in urban centres. So, they created a disincentive for anybody to set up a practice in a city. The government decided that doctors who established themselves in a city would be paid only 80 per cent of what their rural colleagues made. Well, to be frank, I was a young, brown woman in Nova Scotia. I knew that the likelihood of meeting anyone who wanted to settle down and marry me and have kids was pretty remote. But if there was to be any chance at all, I at least had to stay in the urban part of the province.

It took me five years to get a full practice. Then the provincial government changed, and the reform of primary care took hold in Nova Scotia. For the first time it seemed the health care system was going to value us as family physicians and primary care providers, and for a few years I saw things that I can honestly say made my heart sing. The Health Authority established the first Department of Family Practice. We had a conference where they highlighted what family doctors did, and for the first time I saw my colleagues stand up and talk about all kinds of innovative things they were doing in their practices. I spoke, for example, about sharing the responsibility for mental health care, bringing together a team in the family doctor's office—a psychiatrist and a social worker—to transform primary mental health care.

The long-held inferiority complex that we had internalized as the lowest people on the totem pole started to disappear. We were celebrated for our importance as generalists. There was recognition that after the specialist got finished with your heart it was: "Go see your family doctor." If a patient went into the emergency room, and the doctors there said they didn't have a stroke or heart attack and they didn't have a bad infection, they said: "Go see your family doctor. They can sort it out." We began to feel like we mattered. We weren't just little cogs in a giant machine. And it was good for patients, too—patients were put at the centre of everything.

Then the government changed again. It's a sad commentary on democracy in this country that a new government can walk in and simply wipe clean whatever the people before have done, their only motivation, it seems, being their belief the other guys did everything wrong. We watched fifteen years of work get broken down in no time. It is much easier and quicker to destroy than it is to build.

We were aghast, but there was nothing we could do. I was still a very optimistic and idealistic person, and I said, "Well, okay, maybe this is like surfing. You go with the wave and wherever you land is where you land, and each time you just try to get a little ahead." But what the new government put in place was truly shocking, and it started to emerge that they had a very anti-physician approach.

They thought they should leave doctors out of the planning because doctors would be too powerful in the decision-making. It was kind of like building a bridge and saying, "The engineers are too powerful so let's leave them out."

In time the government announced they were going to have meetings all over the province in which they were going to reveal to us what primary care was going to look like in the future. I went into one of those meetings with a group of about a hundred doctors. The way we were spoken to was worse than being told we were slow learners. We were told that we should not even bother renewing the leases on our offices because the world was changing. The world as we knew it would cease to exist.

I won't go into all the details, but their plans were based on faulty or outdated information. They lied about the numbers. For example, they said there were pockets of Nova Scotia that were over-serviced by family physicians. They saw a group of doctors established in one particular area and presumed all their patients lived in that area, which just wasn't true. Anyone who's been a family physician for more than ten years knows that, though their patients grow up and their circumstances change and they move away, they stay with their family doctor. Most of my patients don't live close to my office, so I'm serving a much larger part of the province than the government wants to admit. But by using their faulty data, they could cull the number of family doctors.

Some doctors in that room were crying. We filed out in silence. We had no words. We realized this plan for family physicians would be the final blow. We wrote letter after letter to the government explaining how we saw things, but we were ignored. So, we mounted what I called "the resistance."

I had been in the media quite a bit, so I was asked if I would front our cause. I did two interviews on radio. I said the government was reforming primary care by using a wrecking ball and that it was going to cause absolute chaos and mayhem. I challenged the Minister of Health to a debate. I wanted it in public, moderated by a journalist. I knew that someone like me from the front lines could tell the minister why the reform plan was dangerous to the health care system.

A few months later, it happened. The debate was livestreamed, and it was a landmark. Not that I changed the minister's mind, but for the first time doctors in Cape Breton and outside the main cities heard those of us in Halifax speak about their plight. I knew they were worse off than we were. They were the canaries in the coal mine, and they were on their last breaths. For them to realize that doctors in other parts of the province cared seemed to ignite a spark.

That's when I was glad that I was a doctor. I could speak my truth. Based on all my training and from what I knew of being on the front lines, I knew what was going to happen with this primary care reform. The system was going to lose its ability to help people. Our patients walk through our doors every day in droves and we have to be able to find out, from thousands of people with headaches, which person has the brain tumour. We have to look at the thousands who come in with chest pain and determine who is having a panic attack and who is having a heart attack.

It was our time to rise up and call out to all the other doctors in the trenches. We family physicians are workhorses. Our shoulders droop. Our backs are curved. We're the ones with the big legs and the thick necks, and deep inside we live off the value of the work we do. We don't stand up and shout it from the rooftops, but at least at that point in time I valued myself enough to speak up so we wouldn't be buried alive. Maybe we are like shooting stars, brightest before we disappear.

Do unto Others...

Sheldon Singh

PERHAPS THE MOST COMMON IMAGE WE have of what a heart doctor does comes from television, where cardiologists are often portrayed as heroic figures who swoop into an emergency and save the day. It's not an entirely improbable scenario.

Sheldon Singh is a cardiologist at Sunnybrook Hospital in Toronto. He is, of course, familiar with the TV doctor, but the story he wants to tell is grounded in the day-to-day reality of caring for very sick patients.

I am a cardiac electrophysiologist, a heart rhythm doctor. It's my job to make sure your heart keeps beating—and beating properly. When your heart beats too slowly, I put in a pacemaker to fix it. When it beats too fast, as in atrial fibrillation—the most common arrhythmia in the world, the one that causes strokes—I try to zap out where that's coming from. If you've had a heart attack or a cardiac arrest, I implant a defibrillator in your chest.

The angioplasty doctors are the plumbers of the heart. They find blockages and repair them. Cardiac electrophysiologists like me are the electricians of the heart. We look for the aberrant wiring and get rid of it.

I can tell you a lot of stories about the patients I've done procedures on, saving them from being hospitalized. I love helping these people, I really do. But about six times a year I work in the coronary intensive care unit at the hospital. There are twelve beds there for patients who come into the unit very sick. Some are close to death. This is the unfortunate part about being a heart doctor. When a patient's heart starts to fail, things tend to become critical quickly, so working with these patients is stressful. We do it one week at a time because it's so challenging. To do it more than that would be very difficult, but I find that being on the coronary care unit reminds me that I'm doing what I do for an important reason. It's a humbling week.

Not too long ago when I was on the unit, I had a patient who had bowel issues in addition to his heart issues, and I called a gastroenterologist to help me manage him. He came in around eleven o'clock at night to help me, and he was kind of surprised I was in the hospital so late. I was surprised that he was surprised. He asked me why I was there, and I said, "This is my job. It's my duty. I'm supposed to be here."

After he took care of the patient, we got talking, and I realized he'd been surprised I was still at the hospital because he thought I was an interventional cardiologist. They're the guys who arrive in the midst of an acute heart attack and put stents in and abort heart attacks. They're the doctors you so often see on television, the people who are perceived to save lives, which just goes to show that even within the medical field there's a perception that certain roles are more valuable than others.

After the gastroenterologist had done his job, he went home, but I sat around for another hour or so. There were a couple of things about this patient that were very important. He was a man in his fifties, an immigrant to Canada with two children in their twenties and early thirties. He'd had a cardiac arrest and been down for about half an hour or so. By that I mean he had gone at least thirty minutes without sufficient blood getting to his brain. When you have a cardiac arrest, not enough blood flows from your heart, and the way we compensate for that is by doing cardiopulmonary resuscitation, better known as CPR. If you are given high-quality CPR—someone pushing on your chest properly—you might get sufficient blood flow to your brain. Unfortunately, this man didn't receive CPR quickly, and when he eventually did, it wasn't clear that he received high-quality CPR. Much like the heart, when the brain is starved for oxygen for a period of time, it stops working. And half an hour is a very long time.

This was the second heart attack for this man. He had been successfully treated at another hospital and discharged just two weeks earlier, so you can imagine his family's shock and dismay when it happened again. They couldn't quite comprehend what had happened, and as the hours went by and the patient got sicker and sicker, the daughter seemed to be reacting with disbelief.

I had been at the hospital all day, but from about 6:00 in the evening to 2:00 the next morning I was intensely involved with this one patient. I went home for some sleep and returned at 7:00 a.m.

Nothing earth-shattering happened in all my time with him. There was no emergency surgery. There was no new stent put in. But the job that I did there, the job that took a long time, is why I am a doctor. I had to be attentive to this man. I had to make sure any complications that he had were managed in the best way possible and that he got the best care possible. And the man did survive.

I also had a duty to his children. I had to explain to them what was going on, to brace them for the worst, to make sure they knew exactly why their father was not doing well, what the next steps were and what to anticipate. I do this all the time with families. I sit down with them and I say, "This is a time you want to get your family from Vancouver to fly in to see so-and-so." It doesn't really matter if the patient is a fifty-six-year-old man from an immigrant family or a ninety-seven-year-old woman with children in their seventies. People want to know that someone is looking after their loved one and that they're going to take the time to explain things to them.

When I think about why I do this, I think it's because I want to make sure that, when it's my turn, someone does this for me. You may think that's a selfish way of thinking, but that's how I make sure I'm doing my absolute best. Basically, I am applying a standard to myself that I would expect from everyone else.

I also do this because I wasn't the only guy sitting in the hospital at two o'clock that morning. My second-year resident was there. The nursing staff was there. This is a teaching hospital, and I have to set an example for them. They learn from me and if they learn bad habits, then shame on me. I do things as I do them so the next generation of physicians can see a hard-working Gen-Xer doing his job. I'm hoping that, by seeing my work ethic, they'll understand what it takes to be there for a patient. I don't think it's arrogant of me to think that what I'm doing is the best. I've been very lucky to work with some of the best physicians in Toronto, Boston and New York.

I've had great leaders who showed me how to do things, and I look up to these guys.

I think it's important that I'm not just doing this for me. I'm not doing this just to get a paycheque. I'm not doing this just to be that sensational TV doctor. I'm doing this because a lot of people count on me. The patient is at the centre, of course, but there is family around that patient. There are other health care professionals on the team and I have to be there for them. I have to be there late so another doctor isn't demoralized to think she's the only one coming in at 11:00 at night. I have to be there so my resident knows this is the way you carry on. I have to be there so the family understands what is going on and they know someone is looking after their loved one.

This is why I do this. It's not as sexy a story as the last defibrillator I implanted or the six-hour procedure I did on some very important person. But I look forward to my weeks in the cardiac unit. I rest up for these weeks because they are physically gruelling and emotionally challenging. But they are also extremely satisfying.

"Never Thought We'd See That"

Mike Ertel

ALMOST ANYTHING CAN HAPPEN IN A hospital emergency room. And though no two cases are ever exactly the same, an experienced emergency doctor gets pretty good at knowing what to do when someone comes in with a heart attack or a severe headache or difficulty breathing.

Every once in a while, though, something occurs for the first time— something so unlikely that they've never been trained to deal with it.

Mike Ertel is a doctor of emergency medicine at Kelowna General Hospital. He recalls two cases nothing had prepared him for.

The first story involves my time as an ER doctor in Cornwall, Ontario. That's where I cut my teeth. I'd been there for a while and seen a lot of trauma, but during one of my last weeks there, before I was scheduled to move west to British Columbia, something completely different happened.

It was two o'clock in the morning. When a doctor is working in a smaller centre like Cornwall at that time of the morning, it's not at all unusual for them to be the only doctor in the hospital. The nursery, upstairs, called to tell me that premature twins had been born. The mother had carried them for just twenty-nine weeks, so when she went into labour unexpectedly, they hadn't had time to get her to a bigger hospital in Ottawa. (Typically, doctors would like babies who are born that prematurely to be delivered where they have a neonatal intensive care unit.) I was told that one baby was doing well, but the other had a collapsed lung. It seemed clear to me that someone had to put a chest tube into the lung to get the baby breathing normally. I said, "I'll call the pediatrician."

They said, "We called him and he doesn't feel comfortable dealing with it."

I called the general surgeon. He said, "Mike, I don't feel comfortable with this."

Then I called the anesthesiologist. He said, "I've never done one of these. You go ahead. You're it."

As I went upstairs to the nursery, I was as nervous as I've ever been in my life—petrified, really. I understood why everyone was reluctant. This baby was barely bigger than my hand. The ribs were incredibly small. To surgically insert a chest tube would be very difficult. We didn't even have chest tubes small enough, so I would have to use a feeding tube. The baby's heart was working hard to keep her alive, pumping at 150 beats a minute, which is about 50 per cent faster than normal. That means the ribs were moving at high speed too, and the space I had to hit with the chest tube was very small.

It's not something ER doctors are typically trained to do. I had done the procedure in adults quite routinely, but the closest thing to what I was being asked to do now was in my trauma training when we inserted chest tubes into pigs. The space between their ribs is tiny so it was a good comparison. But pigs aren't human babies, and I had never done this kind of thing under the pressure of life-saving conditions.

I kept looking for excuses not to do it. But it was "Tag, you're it" because I was the only doctor in the hospital. I had to put on my big-boy pants and do it. I thought, if I don't do it, she's dead. Realistically, that child was twenty minutes to a half-hour away from dying. There was no Plan B.

There were about ten of us in the room as we set up for the chest tube. It's really hard to describe how tiny that baby was. I remember bending over her. We had bright lights on. The sweat was pouring off my forehead. I put the tube in as carefully as I possibly could, but I wasn't sure if I was in the right place. Had I managed to get it into her lung?

Then I saw condensation in the tube—breath from the lung! That's when I knew I was in the right place. I'd reached the promised land. The baby went from blue to pink and everybody in the room started applauding. The baby was fine after that. It was a nice save.

Story number two happened one summer day after I arrived in Kelowna. A fifteen-year-old named Marissa was out riding on an ATV with a friend, and their two boyfriends were riding ahead of them on another one. They were going fairly fast up one of the local ski hills. Marissa's friend, who was driving, hit a bump and veered off the trail. Marissa was catapulted into the air and came flying down backwards—right onto a tree. The tree, which was about ten centimetres in diameter, went right through her, just under her diaphragm, and came out near her armpit.

The two guys were so far ahead they didn't even realize what had happened. Marissa's friend wanted to go for help, but Marissa begged her not to go. She said, "I'm dying. Don't leave me."

But her friend said, "No, I've got to go get help." Marissa was left alone, impaled on the tree. She started texting people to say goodbye because she believed she was about to die.

It took the search and rescue team two hours to find her. She was alive, but still skewered, and they could see it would be impossible to lift her into a helicopter with the entire tree, so they would have to shorten it. They started cutting above the armpit and below her tummy. It was a slow process—they had to use a handsaw as the vibrations of an electric saw could have killed her—but eventually they got her up into the helicopter.

We were waiting for her in Kelowna. It's typically pretty chaotic in the trauma room, but this was one of those rare instances when the patient came in and you could have heard a pin drop. Everybody took a step backwards. We took the blanket off this fifteen-year-old girl with a log through her. She was white as a sheet. I honestly thought she was dead.

I leaned in beside her ear and said, "Marissa, I'm Dr. Ertel." I wasn't expecting her to respond so it was a little spooky when she opened her eyes and said, "Hello."

I don't think many of us thought she was going to make it, but we mobilized a team of seven doctors and went to work. The thing that saved her was that the tree had missed her heart by a couple of centimetres. Everything inside her was pressed against the log—that's what was compressing everything and stopping the bleeding. As soon as we took the log out, all hell would break loose, so we wouldn't do that until we got her up into the surgical suite.

When we had everybody ready to take the log out, it was like a symphony. Everybody did a wonderful job. She had a ruptured diaphragm, a bunch of fractured ribs and a collapsed lung. Worse, she had major damage to several internal blood vessels and would bleed out if they weren't repaired quickly enough. It was a bit of a miracle she survived, and even more so that she was out of the hospital in just three weeks. (When she was discharged, she asked me to write a note for school so she could get out of a few things because she still wasn't feeling 100 per cent!)

They say that being an emergency doctor is for adrenalin junkies. Those were two days when I had my fill. But even though experiences like those are rare, I have never left a shift thinking I haven't accomplished something. To see the relief in a family's eyes when you save their loved one? It doesn't get any better than that. I love what I do and find it such a privilege to be part of a team that saves lives. To actually save somebody's life! That's what I'll be thinking about when I'm an old man and retired.

Honesty As Policy

Photo by Nathan Nash

Peter Rosenbaum

EVERY DOCTOR KNOWS THAT NOT EVERY case is going to have a happy ending. Patients know it, too. But there can be some incredibly stressful and uncomfortable moments when doctors can only hope they're finding the right words and expressing the right sentiments to communicate the depth of their concern.

Peter Rosenbaum is a developmental pediatrician and researcher at McMaster University in Hamilton with a special interest in childhood disability. He knows there is no perfect way, and certainly no textbook way, to deliver bad news. But early in his career he found the bedrock to build on.

This story begins when I was an intern at the Royal Victoria Hospital in Montreal. A woman in her early forties was being admitted, and from down the hall I could hear her screaming in agony. It was obvious this was someone in tremendous distress and pain, yet I was supposed to get a history from her. As we spoke, I learned that four months previously she'd had a radical mastectomy. Now she was back in the hospital with excruciating back pain.

After a little while her x-rays were delivered to me. I wasn't trained in radiology, but it didn't take an expert to see that one of the vertebrae in the lumbar area—the lower part of the spine—was not visible. Normally when you look at an x-ray, you can see shadows of varying degrees, but bones look white. I could see very quickly there was a vertebra missing, and it was clear that the cancer had spread. She had significant disease.

She couldn't see my reaction as I looked at the x-ray, but she was very distressed, and she said to me, "The cancer has spread, hasn't it?"

I said, "Yes, it has."

Immediately, I could see the pressure that had built up inside her leaving her body. There was a profound shift in her distress—because someone was being honest with her. We were now able to talk a bit. I found out she had survived Auschwitz. She had met her husband in the camp or soon after she'd been liberated and come with him to Montreal. They had established a flower shop and had children. So, after the incredible abyss she had experienced as a teenager in a Nazi death camp, life had taken a good turn.

But now she was being smacked upside the head with cancer. She had already endured surgery, but now the cancer was back and the prognosis was not good. I spent several days listening to her talk about her life. Everything had changed in our relationship at the moment she'd said, almost in desperation, "The cancer has spread, hasn't it?" and I'd said, "Yes." It helped me realize that being honest with people was actually a good idea. The truth wasn't going to destroy them. Quite the opposite. It was the absence of transparency that was damaging.

Back then I was so young I didn't know enough to lie to her. But I've reflected on this episode a lot in the years that have gone by, and I've recognized that, in addition to the pain that was causing her so much physical distress, this woman was in a profound existential crisis from which she was getting no relief because no one would tell her what was going on. It was a dramatic experience for me both in terms of hearing her in agony from down the hall and having this moment of epiphany with her. The whole tone of our exchange changed deeply. She was obviously still upset, but relieved that somebody had been honest with her after so many people hadn't been. So that experience was profoundly important to me. It showed me the difference between disease and person.

For me, medicine is about individuality. It's about personal issues. Otherwise, your patient is just another gallbladder or cancer.

Now I'm a pediatrician working with childhood disability. Being honest with kids means listening carefully to the questions they ask. There's an anecdote I like to tell to illustrate what I mean. A kindergarten kid comes in and asks her mother, "Where did I come from?" Mommy, who has been ready for this, spends half an hour explaining the gymnastics and biology of reproduction and then says, "I hope that answers your question." And the kid says, "Well, my friend Sarah came from Detroit. Where did I come from?"

So, for years and years I've been teaching medical students to listen to the question and its context. You can ask me, "What is cerebral palsy?" There are only four words in that question, but it can be answered in many ways. None of the answers will be dishonest, but they can be quite different, depending on who's asking the question and why they're asking it.

When a parent asks me, "What does it mean that my child has cerebral palsy?" I try to answer by understanding where the question is coming from. With children it's the same thing—context. Let's say a child has cancer. When I was a medical student back in the sixties, I was taught never to tell a child terrible news. But, of course, children already know when something is off. They see Mommy crying all the time. It was quite remarkable to me even when I didn't know much that you would try to keep this information secret. It was ridiculous. You don't tell the child what the white cells are doing, but you talk honestly to him in a way that is appropriate for his age and stage of understanding. I mean, if you've come to see me and I'm not honest with you, then why would you ever trust me again? Honesty really is a good policy.

I've also learned that truth-telling is a process, not a one-time event. I once had a young patient with Duchenne muscular dystrophy, and back then that was pretty much a death sentence. Today there are treatments that make it better, and patients are living into their twenties, thirties and forties. But not then. So, I was having a conversation with the mother and her husband. He kept asking questions, and as I answered his questions, she progressively turned her chair until she had her back to me. She obviously didn't want to hear this. She wasn't ready. So, part of the art of medicine is the ability to read both the verbal and nonverbal. Most people, when you tell them something serious, have lots of questions. Some of them want to know everything, but others don't.

A doctor's biggest currency is time, and if you have only five minutes in your appointment, it's very hard to have a difficult conversation. I strongly believe in investing time up front in counselling and reviewing things about a patient's predicament because a patient with a reasonable grasp of what's going on is less likely to keep coming back every fifteen minutes. The early investment in time with the family, and even the extended family, is very valuable.

It's inevitable that a doctor will have to deliver bad news. People don't show up at our offices to tell us how well they are or drop in to have a beer. They come to us with problems. That's the nature of our role. So why do we take a blood pressure? Why do we palpate a breast? Why do we do a rectal exam? We're looking for something. What are we going to do if we find something? We have to teach doctors this from the beginning.

One of the things we learn in medical school is that death is the enemy, that it's the worst thing that can happen to you. But as you get older, you recognize a whole lot of things are worse than death. I remember when I was a resident fifty years ago, leukemia was not just going to kill you, it was going to kill you fast. If you had leukemia, you were going to die in six weeks. I found it incredibly distressing. But after a few months I sat in on the disclosure conversations with parents and saw what a good doctor could do. We have to get that wisdom into younger people.

For me, caring, demonstrating a willingness to listen, and trying to help people sort out their physical and existential dilemmas is what medicine is about. Part of that is telling the truth, which is what I first learned all those years ago when I encountered the woman with the back pain. I know that experience made me a better doctor.

Knowing what we have been trained to do—work with people in very difficult circumstances—and then doing it in the most helpful ways is extremely rewarding. There is always a huge amount of suffering in the world. Much of what I try to do, to the very modest extent I am allowed and "empowered" to do it, is relieve a bit of that suffering when people seek my advice. That is what is so rewarding to me about being a doctor.

"I'll Never Forget"

Robin McLeod

IT IS UNSURPRISING THAT IN THE immediate aftermath of a life-saving medical intervention, a patient feels an overwhelming desire to thank the doctor who stepped up in their hour of need. It is more surprising when a patient's thankfulness never fades.

Robin McLeod can attest that those patients do exist. She is a colorectal surgeon in Toronto and a vice-president of Cancer Care Ontario.

It was 1993 and a day of operating for me. Between cases I came down to my office. When I got there, my two secretaries were really energized and happy, and I could tell something was going on. It turned out a florist had delivered a dozen red roses for me. There was a card attached, and it said, "I will never forget you." It was signed, "Marvin."

I was married—to someone *not* named Marvin—and I had two children. I went red in the face when I read the card. I could see my secretaries thinking, this is wonderful. I was thinking hard about who this guy Marvin was, but I had no idea. Then one of the secretaries remembered that earlier in the week someone had phoned to ask for the correct address for my office. I looked at the card for a little while longer, and then I realized who Marvin was.

My mind went back ten years. In 1983, I had just come back to Toronto from a fellowship in colorectal surgery in the US. I was on staff at the Toronto General Hospital and one late afternoon—about five or six o'clock—I was in Emergency when a guy in his early twenties came in. He was in pain and putting out a lot of blood through his stomach. When you see that, the most likely thing that's happened is the patient has an ulcer. It's gone through the duodenum—which is attached to the stomach and sits at the top of the small intestine—and into a blood vessel. At that point, the blood vessel comes apart and the blood won't stop pouring out.

In that situation we would usually do a gastroscopy—that is, we'd put a tube with a camera into his mouth, down his esophagus and into the stomach and beyond to see where the blood was coming from. But we didn't do that in this case because I didn't think there was time to fiddle around. When someone is bleeding that profusely—and he was a healthy young guy—the likelihood of it being something other than a duodenal ulcer or a stomach ulcer is pretty remote. I figured that if we fooled around trying to see exactly where this ulcer was by putting a tube down, we would be wasting time. First of all, there was so much blood it would be hard for us to see anything, and second we would have to open up his abdomen to fix the ulcer anyway. Seeing what was happening and how fast it was happening, we were really scared for him. He was going to bleed to death, so I took him into the OR.

We found the problem very quickly. It was what we thought. He had a bleeding duodenal ulcer, and we repaired it in a couple of hours. It's not a difficult operation, but it saved his life because he was bleeding so much. There was no problem with his postoperative care, and he was discharged in due course.

Now, a decade later, he was sending me roses to mark the tenth anniversary of the day I saved his life. They reminded me of how dramatic Marvin's case had been, and I've always remembered it since then. But after that tenth anniversary surprise I didn't hear anything at all from him for another twenty-five years.

Then on December 7, 2018, Marvin sent me an email. The subject line was: "Thanks for saving my life in 1983. Here's what's happened since."

> *Dear Dr. McLeod,*
>
> *In 1983 you performed a life-saving surgery on me because of a bleeding ulcer that was inconveniently located over a blood vessel. Well, I'm still around and I was thinking about you lately, so I'm writing this short note to say once again thank you for saving my life.*
>
> *I'm living in Vancouver now, married with three grown kids. You might be interested to know that my eldest son has applied for medical school at the University of British Columbia, and he is currently working in Israel at a medical lab doing cancer research. I'm useless on the details, I'm*

afraid, because I went the arts route and picked up a doctor-
ate in art history.

My daughter is attending UBC for political science. My
youngest is in grade 11 and plays high-level soccer and is a
typical teenager. I hope you are well and happy this holiday
season. Thank you for being there for me when I needed you.
Sincerely,
Marvin

The impact you have on patients' lives is what makes medicine so wonderful. It's not that I did something miraculous that some other surgeon couldn't have done. But Marvin needed surgery right away because blood was pouring out of him. I was there and I could fix it. His life was saved, and now three kids are alive as well.

If you were a banker or an accountant and someone wrote to you thirty-five years later, you might say, "I wonder who that guy is." But I'll never forget Marvin. I can still see myself standing in the emergency room with him. I have loved every minute of being a surgeon, and I think we surgeons are lucky because we really do affect patients. If they have a cancer, we take it out. If they're in crisis, we get them past it.

People often love their primary care physicians. Building a long-term relationship with a surgeon is harder. We show up in a life-or-death situation and then move out of a patient's life forever, but I've had lots of patients over the years say to me, "I'll never forget you. I pray for you every night." Or they come to my office and give me a big kiss or a hug. I must say, I love being a surgeon.

A Single Breath

Gil Faclier

NO ONE CAN POSSIBLY PREPARE FOR being hurt in a sudden, unexpected and devastating event when the path of life changes in an instant—literally. The extent of that change is often determined in a hospital.

Gil Faclier is an anesthesiologist at Toronto's Sunnybrook Health Sciences Centre. The image that may pop into your head is that of a doctor in a surgical mask putting you to sleep before an operation. In reality, an anesthesiologist is responsible for everything that maintains normal physiology during surgery: breathing, blood pressure, and the normal function of the heart, kidneys and brain. Dr. Faclier also has a subspecialty as an intensivist, a physician who provides special care for critically ill patients. He remembers a case when one small breath gave cause to celebrate.

In the early eighties when I was in intensive care medicine, a young woman was rushed into the trauma unit of our hospital one night with a severe trauma wound. She had been shot in the neck during a holdup. She was still a teenager, so this was obviously a tragic event. Her arrival immediately triggered the trauma protocol, which meant an urgent page went to all the relevant specialties: anesthesia, neurosurgery, orthopedics, general surgery and the trauma team leader. Once she was stabilized, she was sent straight up to the ICU where she was placed in what is called a "halo frame." This immobilized her neck so the spinal cord wasn't further traumatized by movement.

The higher up an injury is on the spinal cord the more severe the consequences because everything below the injury is impaired. C1 is the highest level on the spine and her neck wound was at level C3 to C4. The injury to the spinal cord was severe—she was essentially paralyzed from the neck down. Complete quadriplegia.

The most immediate problem was her breathing. She was on a ventilator, which means the machine was breathing for her. The challenge was to get her off it and have her breathe for herself. There's a nerve that originates in the neck right where she'd been shot. It's called the "phrenic nerve." If your phrenic nerve doesn't work, your diaphragm doesn't work. And if your diaphragm doesn't work, you can't breathe.

It looked as though we were going to have to put in a phrenic nerve stimulator to get her off the ventilator. It's essentially a pacemaker for the diaphragm. We implant electrodes that stimulate the nerve to make the diaphragm work, but it's complicated because the stimulator is not connecting stationary parts. When you move your neck, your phrenic nerve moves. So, if you can move your neck—and this young woman could—there will be an intermittent loss of contact between the electrodes and the phrenic nerve. If this young woman had to rely on an implant of this kind to breathe, she would be in and out of trouble for the rest of her life, dealing with mechanical failures, battery failures and emergency hospital admissions. The only way that wasn't going to be the case was if she could breathe on her own.

She remained in the ICU for a month or two. That's a long time as long-stay patients run the risk of infection and all sorts of bad things. All this time she couldn't speak. She could only mouth words. I don't know if she understood how dire her circumstances were, but she was very aware of the fact that she wasn't breathing.

When a patient is immobilized 24-7, usually all they can do is think terrible thoughts. But this young woman was a real role model. Everyone on the ward was cheering for her. As time passed, we were becoming desperate, hoping she would start breathing on her own.

And then one morning when I was on rounds, she took a breath. To say it was exciting is not the right word. But it put a lump in my throat. And not just mine. Hers was such a tragic case that this was a cause for the entire intensive care unit to celebrate—all the nursing staff, all of the doctors, all the physiotherapists, all the respiratory therapists. She had become quite a focus. We had twelve to fourteen beds in the ICU, and they were filled with pretty sick people, but her circumstances were the most tragic.

There were lumps in many throats in the ICU when she took that single breath. Of course, that first breath didn't mean she was out of trouble, but she was just an incredible fighter, and her positive attitude blew me away. We couldn't be confident the second breath would follow, but it gave us hope. We knew she was going to be quadriplegic, but she might not need a respirator. If she was always going to need a respirator, she would be more or less institutionalized all her life. If she didn't need a respirator, she would be in a wheelchair but she could have some independence.

At this time, she was still intubated so she wasn't out of the woods yet. That is, there was a tube in her windpipe to keep the airway open and taking that tube out was a bit of a risk. If she failed to breathe now, we would have to put the tube back in, and that would mean moving her neck, which could result in the level of quadriplegia becoming worse. We could do more damage higher up on her spinal cord, causing even more paralysis.

We took the tube out and we all kind of crossed our fingers. Remarkably, she didn't go back into respiratory failure. I say remarkably because of the level of her quadriplegia. Normal breathing is a shared function between the diaphragm and the chest wall, but as she had no function in her chest wall, the breathing mechanics were all different. Her diaphragm had to do it all. A lot of people with respiratory problems can cope because the deterioration in lung function is slow, and the body learns to accommodate. But when the change happens in a heartbeat, you go from entirely normal to entirely abnormal, and the diaphragm has to adapt immediately. Despite all this, she did extremely well.

We kind of kept in contact, which is a little unusual for patients who are discharged from the ICU, and I was pleased to learn that she went on to have a very successful life. Sometimes I remember her and I get a good feeling because I think, yeah, I did a good job.

The Challenge of Uncertainty

Nick Daneman

Photo by Doug Nicholson

IT'S A TERM WE HEAR ALL THE TIME, routinely injected into any conversation about modern medicine: medical science. It may lead us to think about medicine as a pure science like biology, chemistry or physics where hypotheses have been rigorously tested, found to be true and set down as facts in a black and white world.

But medicine isn't pure science. It's applied science. And it's applied to human beings. That means a medical doctor lives in a murky world filled with grey, not black and white.

Nick Daneman is an infectious disease specialist at Sunnybrook Health Sciences Centre (there's that term again) in Toronto. He discovered the difference between medical theory and medical practice on his very first day flying solo.

My father is a doctor, but even with a parent as a physician I don't think I really understood what it meant to be a doctor. At medical school I worked hard. I'm a voracious learner and I always felt I should learn as much as I possibly could so that I would be the best clinician I could be when I graduated. My focus was on the knowledge and the learning, but even the clinical apprenticeship that you do is very different from the moment when you're first working as a practising physician.

My first day as on-call resident was at St. Michael's Hospital in downtown Toronto. It was the Canada Day weekend. I had started my rotation on nephrology because it was one of many potential specialties I was considering. So, I chose to do that first. At that time the resident covered both the inpatient service, which was about twenty or so patients with kidney issues, and a consulting service across the entire hospital for any patient in another ward who developed a kidney problem. For the first time I had ownership of decision-making that was going to directly affect a patient's health. And the biggest surprise of all, I'd say, was doing all that in the face of uncertainty.

In medical school I don't think we appreciated just how much uncertainty there was in practice in terms of patient diagnosis, optimal treatment and prognosis. So it was quite a roller-coaster night for me. I remember how I felt when first the staff doctor and then the senior resident went home. I was left there as a junior—first-year, first-day resident on call. And as I said it was the Canada Day weekend so there really weren't many people around. Pretty lonely.

It got busy almost right away. I got a call about a patient with a blood potassium level of 8. The normal range is from 3.5 to 5, so a blood level of 8 is a serious problem that usually indicates a critical issue with the kidneys. It can result in heart arrhythmias and has to be dealt with as an emergency. I had an approach in my head about what to do for this patient, but of course it was more complex than what you read in a textbook. The patient was in intensive care. He had advanced kidney dysfunction and some other complicating factors. Nothing was textbook, but I managed to get through that.

From then on my pager seemed to ring nonstop and I went from one stressful situation to another. I got a call about a potassium level in the teens, which is not even compatible with life. I rushed down to the ward and was so relieved to discover that the nurse was calling about a urine potassium level rather than a blood potassium level—not nearly as serious.

Then there was somebody with a systolic blood pressure of 220. That's well over the normal range. The patient also had a headache and other symptoms indicative of a hypertensive crisis, which can lead to a stroke. I remember writing the antihypertensive prescription and for the first time recognizing there wouldn't be anybody following up my prescription with a co-signature. My drug treatment was going to be the final word. It gave me pause: Was I sure it was the right drug and the right dose?

It went on and on like that through the night. Each emergency call may have been something I had read about and felt comfortable with from a knowledge basis, but to act and take ownership of the situation and to do that in an urgent emerging fashion in the face of uncertainty was a challenge I remember to this day.

At about 9:00 p.m. it suddenly occurred to me that I hadn't eaten for half a day. All the cafeterias were now closed and I couldn't leave the hospital because I was on call. My only choice for food was on the main level of the hospital, where there was a Second Cup coffee shop. They had what must have been a day-old package of cold noodles, which I ate before rushing off to another ring of my pager.

This time I was informed that unfortunately a patient had passed away unexpectedly. They needed me to pronounce death.

I remember thinking in a panic that I'd never learned how to pronounce death. What was I supposed to do? Could I look this up in a book? Then I said to myself: Wait a second. This is the first person I've seen tonight that I can't actually do harm to. That calmed me down.

Somewhere around 5:00 a.m. I had a chance to lie down. I had started my shift twenty-one hours earlier and I still had seven hours ahead. On the nephrology ward at that time, they didn't even have a separate call room where the resident could sleep. Instead they had refashioned one of the dialysis rooms as a resident call room, which kept residents close to the action. This meant I could still hear all the beeping of the patients' monitors, and there was also a patient across the hall with advanced dementia who was calling out, "Hello-o-o-o-o!" at the top of her voice over and over again. I was just falling asleep at about 5:30 in the morning when my pager went off again.

This time I was told there was a kidney available for transplant. Somebody who had signed up as an organ donor had died somewhere in the Toronto area, and I had to find the patient who was going to receive a new kidney. That kind of blew me away because, as a resident on my first day on call, I was going to be completely responsible for organizing a kidney transplantation. It was my responsibility to get out the transplant list to see who was at the top and get that person to the hospital. All the people who had been waiting desperately for organ replacements were on the list, and there was a pager number to reach each of them. I called the number for the man at the top of the list and then waited for him to call back. Time was ticking by, he wasn't returning the page, and all I was thinking was how awful it would be for this person not to get his kidney transplant.

I waited as long as the protocols allowed, but he didn't call back, so I paged the next person on the list. That was a high point of the roller-coaster ride I was on—getting through to that person and telling him that there was a kidney available for him. He rushed to the hospital, and I met him and his family. He was all teed up for his transplant, and it was successful. The person who had been at the top of the list called back the next day. He said his pager had been in the trunk of a car, so he hadn't heard it. He was disappointed, of course, but at least he was still at the top of the list and hoping he could get a transplant soon.

At the end of that night I was completely exhausted. It had been a twenty-eight-hour mix of anxiety, frustration, hunger, pride and exhilaration. I had absorbed the full impact of what it meant to be a physician, a perspective you just can't pick up in medical school. I had done calls as a student, but there was always somebody overseeing me, and I had never been left in a position of major responsibility. I learned that night what it really meant to be a doctor. I also got a sense of why I was a doctor.

There were a few more nights like that in my training. Sometimes they were crushing, and I went home feeling sad because of the patients I couldn't help. Sometimes I went home frustrated about situations where I didn't have enough information to know the best approach to take. And sometimes I went home feeling exhilarated because I had been able to help people. But that first night was a real lesson in uncertainty. Prelearned knowledge on medical topics is helpful. Targeted reading and consulting colleagues are also important. But in the end, there is always uncertainty. During residency, I tended to revere and mimic the confident consultants, the ones who delivered definitive advice without hesitation. But over time I really grew to admire the questioning consultants—the doctors who delivered cautious advice, who openly deliberated, who identified uncertainty and acted in the face of this uncertainty to deliver optimal care for their patients.

In hindsight, one of the reasons I can say, "That's why I'm a doctor" is that I've come to embrace the challenge of this uncertainty, to think in terms of probabilities rather than binary "yes" and "no" answers. I'm able to act on the best evidence even when it's not perfect evidence. I've learned to see uncertainty from the patient's side of things, too. I'm sure people suffering from illnesses often aren't aware of the kind of uncertainty that surrounds their diagnosis, so I think it's important to communicate that to patients. It's also what has drawn me to the job description of clinician scientist, splitting my time today between active clinical care and active research. That's how I can explore the unanswered questions of how best to diagnose and treat patients with infectious diseases, working to advance knowledge and perhaps reduce uncertainty.

"This Is Badass!"

Donna May Kimmaliardjuk

MOST OF US HAVE LEARNED TO appreciate that anyone called "doctor" is well educated, wise, maybe even brilliant. We give little thought to where they came from or the path they took to get where they are.

Donna May Kimmaliardjuk started life in a small Inuit community in Nunavut. She is Canada's first Inuk heart surgeon, now the chief resident in cardiac surgery at the University of Ottawa Heart Institute. There's usually a special burden on any "first" in any field, and it's no different in medicine. But accolades and praise are no substitutes for doing the job, and there comes a time when your abilities are put to the test.

It was a Sunday afternoon in July. I had been a fourth-year resident in heart surgery for just a couple of weeks. I was done seeing patients for the day but I was on call, which meant I was in the hospital to look after the forty to fifty patients recovering from cardiac surgery, just in case any trouble popped up.

I was sitting at my desk on the second floor of the hospital doing some paperwork when I heard an urgent call over the intercom.

"Code Red H3. Code Red H3."

That indicated fire on the third floor. That sounds scary, but I didn't think much about it. It usually meant someone had left their lunch in the microwave too long or someone had been smoking too close to a smoke detector. But it was a little weird because when there's a Code Red lights are supposed to start flashing, and that wasn't happening. I thought, this doesn't make any sense. I sat there and wondered: Should I go up? It's only one floor above me.

I found out later that a relatively new operator got her codes mixed up. Suddenly there was a new call.

"Code Blue H3."

Code Blue means a patient's heart has stopped and he's not breathing. It came over the intercom just once. That was even weirder, because any Code Blue gets called out four times. It's supposed to be very loud and my pager should have gone off too, but it didn't.

I thought, what the heck is going on? I decided I had better go up to see for myself. When I arrived at the nursing station on the third floor there was no one there. It was quiet—again a weird circumstance. Then I saw a nurse running out of a patient's room. She saw me and said, "They're doing CPR on a surgery patient. He has no pulse."

I ran into the room and knew immediately that the patient was a man in his mid-seventies who'd had open-heart bypass surgery four days earlier. In fact, I had seen him that morning because I was somewhat worried about him. I had been called to see him on Friday night about his breathing. When I came back on Sunday morning I purposely went in to see how he was doing. At that time, he looked well. I told him, "You're on the right track. I'm really happy with your progress."

Now, just a few hours later, he was dying. An anesthesiologist was trying to give him oxygen to get him breathing. A staff cardiologist and a cardiology fellow were doing CPR. An anesthesia fellow was trying to get an IV into him to give him drugs that might get the heart going again. And, of course, there were nurses everywhere. A Code Blue always produces a big scene with everybody working under tremendous stress.

Now I arrived. I was the most junior person in the room, but because the patient had had heart surgery, he was my responsibility. I thought, oh god. But everyone was very supportive, and they let me lead. In fact, no one else knew as much about heart surgery as I did. The cardiologist doesn't do surgery. The anesthesiologist doesn't do it either.

I got in touch with the staff surgeon, who was not in the hospital. He said, "Donna, what's going on?" I gave him the story. By now the doctors had been doing CPR for about ten minutes. I said we'd keep going and he said, "Okay, call me back in five minutes with an update."

Another five minutes went by and there was still no heartbeat or blood pressure. I had just read guidelines a few weeks before about what to do when a patient is recovering from open-heart surgery and his heart stops. The guidelines said you should open him up. You need to physically see inside and figure out what's not working. Is there bleeding? Is the pacemaker malfunctioning? Is it something else?

I had never done that before—opened up a patient by myself, let alone in a patient's room rather than an operating room. It's an uncontrolled environment. It's not sterile. I didn't have a surgeon or assistant to help me. It was just me. But I knew this was what I had to do.

We got the staff surgeon back on the phone and I told him, "It's been fifteen minutes. There's no heart rate. I'm opening him in his room. You need to come in and we'll take him to the OR. But I'm opening him up here."

He said, "Okay, Donna."

When I told everyone what we were going to do, they were amazing. No one questioned my decision. I quickly got into a sterile gown and gloves. A nurse grabbed some alcohol solution and poured it over the patient's chest to disinfect it. The doctors continued with the CPR until I was ready.

We had a very basic tray of instruments. The scalpel was in my hand. The moment I started to cut was like a movie. Even though I know there was a lot of commotion, it seemed that everything went quiet and changed into slow motion. I cut through the skin. There was still no heartbeat or blood pressure. I had doctors on each side of the patient feeling for a pulse in the patient's groins, but they didn't feel anything yet.

At the end of any open-heart surgery the patient's chest is closed with stainless steel wires that go through and around the breastbone. I'm not a very big person and not particularly strong and the wires can be really tough to put in and take out. But I knew I now had to cut through them.

I took the wire cutter and started to cut the wires to open the breastbone. As I cut the second wire, the chest moved. One of the doctors said, "I have a pulse." Even now as I remember it, I can feel my heart rate rising and I'm getting goosebumps.

I exhaled and said, "Okay."

I cut the rest of the wires and was able to pull them out. I still needed a clear view to figure out what had caused the heart to stop. Was there something I could fix? When I was opening him up, I'd anticipated finding blood in his chest. Bleeding is one of the most common causes for the heart to stop. All the blood accumulates in the chest until the pressure becomes so great that it compresses the heart until it can't beat anymore. Expecting to find that, I'd asked the nurses to have saline ready to pour into the chest to clean it out so I could see what was going on. But now that he was open, I didn't see any bleeding. I didn't see anything out of the ordinary.

The staff surgeon arrived. He had a quick look and he said, "I don't know what's wrong here. Let's get him down to the operating room."

The patient's chest was still open. I had some sterile towels and I was trying to cover his chest and hold it together with these towels. I stood beside him like that as we wheeled his bed down the hall, into the elevator and finally into the operating room.

The nurses in the OR had no idea what was going on. When they saw me, one of them said, "Oh my god, you have his chest open."

I said, "Yes, it's a true emergency. We've got to go."

We got him on the table and had a look. Thankfully the bypasses were working well. There was no damage from the CPR or from when I opened him.

We concluded that something was wrong with the pacemaker, or with the wires attaching the pacemaker to his heart. We replaced everything, closed his chest again and brought him back to the intensive care unit. In due time he woke up normally. No stroke. No brain damage. The best result possible.

We had a man who was dying. He had no blood pressure and no heart rhythm. I'm not sure even today why his heart started beating again. They were giving him drugs through the IV and maybe the drugs finally kicked in at the same time I was cutting the wires in his chest. Or maybe his brain was feeling the pain of his chest being opened and that was enough to get the heart going. I'm not sure. Had I not reopened, I could have been criticized by colleagues because I wouldn't have followed the guidelines to reopen the chest with someone so soon after surgery because there could be something that you can only address by physically having your hands in there.

I spoke to the surgeon who did the original open-heart surgery and he said, "Donna, you saved his life."

That's the day I felt: This is badass. This is why I do what I do. From that day on I felt I have what it takes to be a heart surgeon.

Prolonging Death

Rebecca Rodin

WE HAVE REACHED AN ERA WHEN IT IS possible to keep a person alive far beyond the point where nature has already surrendered. Mostly, that is good. But more and more we are realizing there can be a dreadful price to pay for more time. It's certainly one of the most challenging dilemmas in modern medicine.

Rebecca Rodin is at the beginning of her career as an internal medicine resident working mostly at Mount Sinai and Toronto General hospitals. She has already seen patients who think certain measures that are meant to prolong their lives are really just prolonging their deaths.

At this stage of my career I spend a lot of time in the emergency room, where a very broad spectrum of cases come my way. A case can be acute and life-threatening, or it can be a more socially determined component of health like being unable to function properly at home, or like falling, which is a common problem among older people living alone.

One fairly busy night, a lady that we can call Margaret came into the emergency department. She had been seen in previous emergency department visits because she had suffered some falls. But she was different from the people I usually see about falling because she was much younger—just in her mid- to late fifties. It's usually a much older population that comes in after falling, so this visit surprised me a bit.

Although Margaret had a history of falls, there had been no clear diagnosis. She also had unexplained bloating and nausea, which had not been intensely investigated. We did a preliminary examination, and before too long we could tell she had some kind of malignant process in her abdomen—some kind of cancer that was causing lots of fluid retention in her belly. It turned out there was a large mass pressing on her spinal cord and causing the decreased sensation in her legs. There was also what we call "saddle anesthesia," which is the loss of sensation around the area of your body that would sit on a saddle—the inner thighs, rectum, perineum and genitals. People with saddle anesthesia generally say they can't feel any sensation, so they have bowel and bladder problems, and they can have difficulty walking. Ultimately, if left untreated, it can cause paraplegia as well, so it is a medical emergency.

Margaret was a young woman—or at least young by my standards. She had a husband and children. She was active and working. She had come to Emergency thinking this was something relatively benign. She had just felt under the weather and didn't know what to make of it, but she didn't have any suspicion that anything more sinister was going on. Now we found out she had cancer.

It's a wonder how many times I've had to diagnose cancer in the emergency department. While many cancers are diagnosed on routine screening or by the family doctor or an oncologist, it's not an infrequent experience for me to have these new cases turn up in the emergency room. But as I said, it was a busy night in Emergency. It was winter flu season, and that had brought in more people than usual, so it was crowded. That meant Margaret was in a bed in the hallway, which is not a great place to have an intimate conversation, but there were no private rooms available. I had to give her this terrible news, all this information about what we had found, and try to present some plan for treatment. It would be an understatement to describe these conditions as suboptimal. She really stuck with me, though. She had a sweet demeanour and strong sense of purpose as I broke the news to her. It's kind of a weird thing to say that you enjoy being a doctor at a time like this, but there's something satisfying in being with people during difficult periods of their lives and helping them navigate the way forward.

The default position for me with a newly diagnosed cancer patient is to start making plans for biopsies and tests, especially for a relatively young person like Margaret. In a more elderly, frail person there's a much greater chance that they may not want treatment. It's common to hear people say, "Do everything you can to keep me alive as long as possible." But sometimes people say, "Listen, I just want to go home. Let me enjoy the time I have left with my family. I don't want to suffer."

Margaret's case had two aspects to it. First, she had an important medical emergency—the compression of her spine, which if left untreated could cause paralysis in her legs. We could do something about the mass on her spine with radiation and steroids, which would both prolong her life and improve her quality of life. She readily agreed to that.

But the second aspect was the main cancer. Most likely it was some kind of gynecologic tumour, but we would have to do more testing to find out, and we already knew it was seriously advanced. I laid out the options for her. It was then up to her to determine whether she wanted to investigate her cancer or just be sent home and kept comfortable. She opted not to pursue any invasive diagnostic tests or potentially life-prolonging but toxic therapies. Are you willing to undergo invasive and sometimes harmful treatments to prolong the length of your life at the expense of your quality of life? It's a very personal decision.

After Margaret had made her decision, I saw her with her very supportive and loving family. It was particularly heartbreaking. We sent her home, promising to do everything possible to keep her comfortable for as long as possible. We arranged for home nursing and some home visits by a physician. We gave her applications for hospices and palliative care units in case home care became too difficult to manage.

I found it satisfying to coordinate Margaret's care at home and make sure she could have her wishes fulfilled. As a doctor I had used my diagnostic skills in an intellectually stimulating fashion, but I had also helped Margaret and her family cope during a life-altering and life-limiting time. It was challenging, to be sure, but it was also very meaningful.

Looking Outside
the Box

Michael
Charness

IT'S AN EXPERIENCE EVEN THOSE OF US
who aren't doctors have had. We're
working hard, doing everything right—
yet still the situation we're dealing
with isn't getting better. In fact, it's
getting worse.

That's a situation Michael
Charness faced as a young resident.
Today he is a neurologist at Boston
and Harvard Universities and works in
the U.S. Veterans Affairs health care
system. He recalls a case that drove
him to the point of exhaustion and
forced him to think more creatively
than he ever had before.

The patient was a sixty-seven-year-old woman. For six weeks before she was admitted to the hospital, she had experienced knee and hip pain, severe headaches, fever and fatigue. She had lost some weight as well. Then ten days before she was admitted, she started having short episodes of blurred vision. The diagnosis was giant cell arteritis.

Even today we're not sure what causes it, but we know it's an autoimmune disease in which the body's immune system attacks and inflames the arteries. It can attack any of the arteries, even the aorta—the largest one in the body—but more commonly it involves the arteries at the side of the head, near the temples. One of the most feared complications of the disease is blindness.

When this woman was admitted to the hospital, we already knew what was wrong with her. She was being treated for arteritis with steroids, which was the standard treatment. But in the midst of her treatment she had developed an occlusion of the central retinal artery—that is, the artery that is critical to the blood supply to the retina had become blocked, and this blockage had caused her to lose much of the vision in both of her eyes. I am not an ophthalmologist, but because I was a medical intern at Johns Hopkins Hospital, I was responsible for her overall care. And I could use a basic ophthalmoscope, the hand-held instrument anyone who's ever been to the eye doctor will recognize, to look at the blood vessels in her eyes. I could see little trains of red blood cells chugging along, stopping and starting. It was very easy to appreciate that blood wasn't getting through.

Since steroids were no longer helping this patient, we rushed her over to a nearby eye institute where they had her inhale carbon dioxide. It's a way to make blood vessels relax, which of course would allow blood to flow freely, and she had temporary relief. However, it's very difficult to get people to continue breathing carbon dioxide because it makes them feel like they're suffocating. So, this was a very short-term treatment that was only briefly helpful and not at all sustainable.

The ophthalmologist then had another suggestion. He told me I could very gently rub on her eyelids to massage the outer cornea and force fluid from the eyes. This would reduce the pressure in the eye so that the blood trying to get into the eye through the blood vessels could get through more easily.

I did exactly what he said: I started rubbing her eyes every hour, and it worked. I could look into her eyes with my ophthalmoscope and see an increase in the blood flow. The effect was dramatic. I would rub her eyes and her vision would improve from say 20/80 to 20/60—a noticeable improvement. The problem was that the effect wore off within sixty minutes.

In those days, residents did a three-day cycle: on the first day, we were up all night; on the second day, we were up most of the night; on the third day, we went home at 11:00 p.m. That meant I was at the hospital a lot of the time, and every hour I would run back into her room and massage her eyes. But of course, I had a slew of other patients to take care of besides this woman, so I was doing this kind of three-ring circus, and by the second day I was running out of steam. Every hour, I ran to do the eye massages and check to see that there was improvement in the pressure in her eyes and in her vision. I did this without any sleep for forty-eight hours straight. I knew this wasn't sustainable. It was working, but it wasn't possible to keep treating her this way indefinitely. Yet we knew that if we stopped the massages and did nothing else, this woman was going to become blind. Irreversibly. If she lost her vision, there would be no getting it back.

That was when I thought about nitroglycerine. You put it under your tongue for chest pain when you have narrowing of the arteries in your heart because nitroglycerine dilates blood vessels. It hadn't been used for arteritis, but I was pretty desperate. This woman wasn't having chest pains, but we thought maybe this would help relax the blood vessels in her eye and allow just enough blood to get through. By this time her eyesight had deteriorated to the point that she had barely discernible vision in both eyes. She was on the verge of becoming permanently blind, so I put some nitroglycerine under her tongue and then took out my ophthalmoscope and watched. Sure enough, I could see it happening. The blood that had been moving so slowly, stopping and starting, suddenly picked up. There was almost normal blood flow in her eyes. Within about thirty minutes her vision improved again to about 20/40.

We followed up on the nitroglycerine under the tongue by putting a nitroglycerine patch on her arm so it could be absorbed gradually through the skin. That worked too. We didn't have to massage her eyes anymore. The blood kept flowing; her vision was restored and sustained.

She was still good forty-eight hours later. She was still good seventy-two hours later. And she was good going forward. We had been frank with her as we were going through the different treatments, explaining what was happening—what we were trying to do and what we were trying to prevent. She understood the stakes were high. Once we could safely tell her she wasn't going to be blind, she was of course very grateful.

I was completely exhausted. But we'd had this moment, this dramatic moment when out of desperation we had tried something different and it had actually worked. It allowed a woman who was going blind to continue seeing. It was one of the most remarkable experiences of my career, and certainly it was very formative because it was so early in my career. I realized then what it means to be a doctor. My profession was going to give me the ability to do things that would have an impact on the lives and wellness of other human beings. You don't forget a case like that. I've never forgotten that woman and the impact that moment had on both of us.

"What Happened to You?"

Felice Lackman

NO SURGERY IS RISK-FREE. IN SOME RARE cases even those operations that we have come to call "routine" or "minor" can have devastating unintended consequences. Every surgeon wants to eliminate, or at least minimize, preoperative conditions that are likely to make a procedure more difficult.

Felice Lackman is a gynecological oncologist at Markham Stouffville Hospital, north of Toronto. Her talk with a patient about risk changed that patient's life.

I deal with women with gynecological cancers. About five years ago a lady, about fifty years old, came to me after she had been diagnosed with endometrial cancer. This type of cancer—cancer of the lining of the uterus—is the most common gynecological cancer, but fortunately it's also the most treatable one.

Endometrial cancer happens most often in women who are overweight, so it's never a surprise when a woman with this disease arrives in my office carrying a few extra pounds. But the woman in front of me on this day weighed almost four hundred pounds— she was morbidly obese. She was wearing an old lady's housecoat because no other clothes would fit her. That's how big she was.

There was no doubt she needed surgery. She needed her uterus removed—a hysterectomy. She had been to see a few other doctors before me, but nobody wanted to operate on her because she was so big, which meant the chances of surgical complications were very high.

She faced multiple problems due to her weight, the first being anesthetic risk. It would be hard to find veins to deliver the anesthesia intravenously, hard to determine the right dose of medication, hard to make sure she was getting enough oxygen and hard to place a breathing tube. It would also be a more technically difficult surgery because we would have to go through all those layers of fat, which would increase the chance of bleeding, and she would be at very high risk for infection. Afterwards she would be at high risk of getting a pulmonary embolism—a blood clot in an artery between the heart and the lungs. Her weight would also slow her healing and decrease her mobility. Compared to someone who wasn't obese, she had a much greater risk of dying.

So, I sat down with her and I said, "Listen, you need to have surgery. We have to take your uterus out because you have cancer, and I am going to do the surgery. It's all booked. But you need to do something for me before we do this."

She said, "What do I have to do?

I said, "You need to lose at least twenty pounds."

Of course, twenty pounds wasn't at all significant in the grand scheme of things. It was just a starting point. It was getting her to look at herself in the mirror and change her lifestyle. In all good con-science I couldn't tell her I wasn't going to operate until she lost a hundred pounds because it seemed unlikely she would do that. But I said, "You need to lose twenty. You need to start losing weight. Not because of the cancer. You have to lose weight just for your general health."

Her eyes bugged out and she said, "How do I do that?"

I said, "You start by getting up off the couch and just stop eating as much."

I don't think she was very impressed with this as I'm sure I wasn't the first person to tell her she had to lose weight. But maybe everyone else had told her she had to lose a lot of weight, and I was giving her a goal she might be able to achieve. Besides, even if she could lose all that weight, it would take some time; it would be impossible for her to lose it all before I did the surgery. If I waited a year to operate, the cancer could have spread, and her life would have been compromised.

The problem with endometrial cancer, from a surgical point of view, is that it's always better to operate on people who are fit and not overweight. They do better because they don't have all those increased risks. That suggests I should have taken my time and let her lose a few pounds first. But from a cancer point of view, the worry is that it could start to spread and eventually kill the patient. With endometrial cancer that's not very common, but it can happen. So that suggests the sooner you operate the better.

I chose to do the surgery because she needed it, even though she had lost just a few pounds by then, and it went well. She didn't have any complications. She went home, and I saw her six weeks later for the usual follow-up. She was doing just fine, and I thought that was the last we would ever have to do with each other. But about a year later, a woman I didn't recognize came into my office without an appointment. She said, "Dr. Lackman, I don't think you remember me."

I looked at her closely and I had no idea who she was. I normally recognize my patients. I might not know their names, but I'll know if I have seen them before. Not this time. I said, "I'm sorry. I really don't remember you."

She said, "I'm Mrs. Sanders. I was here a year ago."

I looked at her again. As I began to recognize her, my eyes must have been as big as Frisbees and my mouth was probably hanging open—the weight loss was that dramatic. I blurted out, "Wow, what happened to you?"

She said, "After you told me I needed to lose weight, something just clicked. I joined Weight Watchers after the surgery. I've lost a lot of weight. I feel great, and I wanted to thank you." She handed me a card and a gift.

I said, "I don't need a card or a gift because losing weight is the best thing you could have ever done for yourself, and I am just happy that I could have been such a positive influence on you." But after she left, I opened the card, and it was this beautiful handwritten thank you:

Dear Dr. Lackman,

You changed my life and I would like to thank you. Last summer when you told me you would be doing my surgery, you also told me, "It's your job to lose weight." Although I didn't lose much before surgery (which will have been one year ago this Thursday), your words stuck with me. After recovering from surgery, I joined Weight Watchers online and in 39 weeks I have lost 110 pounds.

Although I still have a long way to go, I wanted you to know that I'm working on the "job" you gave me. Next year my husband and I will be celebrating our 40th wedding anniversary. We will be taking a transatlantic cruise that will end in London where we plan to stay for a few days. My goal is to be under 200 pounds. I'm also challenging myself to participate in the Terry Fox Run next year.

Without you I couldn't have fathomed myself doing these things. Saying "thank you" seems so inadequate, but I will say it anyway. Thank you for changing my life.

This is why I'm a doctor, I thought. Not because I can cut people open. Not because I can take out their cancers. But because as a doctor I can influence someone for the better.

He Was Supposed to Die

Sam Campbell

DOCTORS WILL TELL YOU THAT EVEN IN the emergency room most of their patients aren't close to the edge of death—though sometimes they really are.

Sam Campbell is chief of emergency medicine at Halifax Infirmary, the major trauma centre in Nova Scotia. He has a vivid recollection of saving a life one night, but even in that moment of triumph he couldn't escape memories of patients he couldn't save.

It happened one night about ten years ago. It was a busy night, and it got busier when, at about 2:00 a.m., the paramedics rushed in with a young man in his early to mid-twenties. They had picked him up outside a bar where he had been in some kind of fight. He had been stabbed in the chest by something very narrow, which I thought might have been a thin screwdriver or an ice pick. Someone had punched him in the chest with it, and I could clearly see two or three holes. One blow had hit his heart.

He was just lying there on the table. Normally with trauma it's ABC: open an Airway, get the patient Breathing, and look after blood Circulation. I realized this young man didn't have any circulation, and his blood pressure was negligible. I could see that the veins in his neck were filling with blood, which told me that his heart had pretty much stopped working: blood was getting to the veins but it was blocked there so it wasn't returning to his heart.

The heart, which sits in a bag called the "pericardium," is essentially two pumps. The right ventricle pumps blood into your lungs, where it picks up oxygen. That blood then goes to the left side of your heart and gets pumped around your body. But in this case, the right ventricle had been punctured, so the blood wasn't going to the lungs. Instead, it was just being pumped out into the bag around the heart. As the bag filled with blood, it put pressure on the heart, to the point that it couldn't pump any longer. The first thing that happens in a situation like this is the blood pressure drops. The patient loses consciousness because there's no blood flowing through the head. The veins in the neck start swelling because the blood in them can't get back to the heart because the heart's not able to pump. It didn't take me long to realize that all this was happening.

When you have a major trauma in a hospital, a whole bunch of people are paged to come down to Emergency to help. But on this night, things moved so fast that no one had arrived before I decided to act. It was just me, the paramedic who'd brought him in and a young resident doctor. There was a kit in front of me with a very small scalpel in it. It was different from the kind of scalpel I would normally use—the blade was probably just a centimetre and a half long, so small it's usually used just to make a little hole in the skin to put in an intravenous line. But it was the only scalpel available, so I grabbed it and basically slashed the patient's chest open. I saw immediately that I was right. The sac around the heart was filling with blood—what we call a "hemopericardium"—so I cut the bag open to evacuate the blood. Now I could see the hole in his ventricle, and I put my finger on the hole to stop the blood from flowing out of his heart into the bag. This allowed his heart to pump normally, restoring the normal flow, and I could actually feel his heart fill with blood.

Within a few seconds he started waking up. He hadn't had any medication or sedation, and he didn't realize what was going on, so he was trying to sit up while I had my hand in his heart. The paramedic gave him some drugs to knock him out and I got the resident to put his finger in the hole so we could intubate (put a breathing tube down his throat). The resident held his finger there as the patient was taken to the operating room where a cardiac surgeon was waiting.

And then it was over for me. Of course, there was blood everywhere to be cleaned up, but I just went back to my job. I picked up the next patient, who happened to be the bouncer from the nightclub where the scrap had happened. During the fight, he had been hit with a bottle and it had cut his head open. So, I was sewing up this guy's head, which was kind of surreal because he was describing what had happened from his point of view, though he had no idea what had happened to the kid we had just dealt with.

It was a weird night.

I had done the procedure that I performed on that young man a few times before, but this one seemed different. I had trained in South Africa, where stabbings happen relatively often, but in my Canadian experience it was not common. When the stabbing results in a hemopericardium, the survival rate is very low. Really, this young man was just lucky. He had managed to get to the hospital while his heart was still working, so when he got into serious trouble, he was in the right place—a trauma centre. I wouldn't have been surprised if he'd died. Given the circumstances, you could say he was supposed to die.

The usual profile of stabbing victims involves the drug trade or some other criminal enterprise—the joke is that the life you save today might take your life tomorrow—but it turned out this young guy was a student. His girlfriend had gone out with some friends while he'd stayed at his university residence to study. He went to pick her up and just happened to be outside this nightclub when trouble erupted. He was just a good Canadian kid.

For a couple of days, I became a minor celebrity. I went and visited him in the hospital but he didn't remember anything. There were so many doctors wandering around him going, "Oo-ooh" and "a-ah" that I just felt a bit awkward and didn't tell him who I was. The hospital foundation, which uses happy stories to encourage donations, asked me if I would approach him to see if he would let us use his story as a fundraising tool, and I couldn't do that.

I reflected later that it's a really difficult decision to grab a scalpel and cut someone's chest open. Part of you is thinking: What if I'm wrong? What if this isn't what I think it is? I don't think about this case every day. The things I think about every day are the times that ended with a patient dying. They are the times I wonder if I did something too early or too late, or if I did something I shouldn't have done.

I once treated a young girl who had a headache. It had all the features of a relatively benign headache caused by irritation of the nerves that come out of the base of the skull. It causes a shooting pain over the front of the head, kind of like a tension headache. I injected a local anesthetic into the area the nerve comes from. That relieved her symptoms and she went home. But a week later I found out she was dead. The cause of her headache had been more serious, something I had never seen in my twenty years of medicine at that time. So, part of me thinks you can't investigate every benign headache as if it were the worst-case scenario because unnecessary tests and treatments could do more damage in the long run. But when I finish making excuses, I'm left with the bottom line—she came to me for help, I missed it, and she's dead. And I ask myself: What if someone else had been there? Would they have picked it up? Did I stop thinking too early?

When something like this goes wrong for any of us, all our friends will try to cheer us up. They'll say, "You did what everyone would have done. That could have happened to any one of us. There was absolutely no way you could have avoided it." But I'll still be saying to myself, it was my job, and I screwed up.

In emergency medicine you get an incredible amount of information thrown at you. Almost every patient is someone I've never met before. They tell me a bunch of things, some of which are what we call "signals," and it's really important to hear these things. But a lot of what they say is "noise"—it's irrelevant. So, we try to work out what is a signal and what is noise—what to focus on and what to ignore.

One of the reasons I hesitate to recount my success story is that when I start thinking of that one case where everything worked out perfectly, I immediately start thinking of the times when things ended badly. I'm reminded that I'm not as hot as I think I am. I may have saved one, but that gets balanced on the other side. But that night with the young man who had the hemopericardium—that was probably the most dramatic thing I've ever done. That story sticks with me as the crowning episode of my career. That's the difference I wanted to make as a doctor.

A Real Eye-Opener

Howard Lewis

IT'S NOT HARD TO FALL INTO A RUT when most of what you do seems routine, and you've been doing it for a long time.

Howard Lewis graduated as an optometrist from the University of Montreal in 1968, so he's been in practice for more than fifty years. Not too long ago, he challenged himself to do something he'd never done as an optometrist, and he's glad he did.

One of my heroes is my dad, who was also an optometrist. He started practising in 1939 and, believe it or not, he didn't retire until he was ninety-three years old. He was working two days a week at that age. He enjoyed his work and it prolonged his engagement with life. I get a lot of inspiration from my father, and I'm sure I'll continue working well into my eighties.

I'm obviously not dealing with life-and-death situations, but I get a lot of satisfaction helping people to see better. It opens their world. I also get a lot of satisfaction seeing an eye disease and referring the patient to have it checked out. It's especially gratifying when someone comes back and says, "I went in to see the ophthalmologist on your recommendation, and he found something, and I want to thank you very much for referring me. The problem has cleared up and everything is now fine. So, thank you."

When I finished school, the scope of optometry was very narrow. We concentrated on tests to get the right prescriptions for glasses or contact lenses. We didn't delve into diseases. If we saw disease or suspected disease, we sent the patient to an ophthalmologist. But over time the scope of optometry has enlarged, and in 2000 I took a special course to learn dilation. It's a procedure that involves putting drops of medication into a patient's eyes. The drops force the muscles that control the opening of the iris to relax. The pupils get larger so it's possible to see inside. So, I got my credentials and a licence to use these diagnostic drugs. But then I backed off and didn't do it. No particular reason. I just didn't do it.

Fifteen years later though, a good friend, a family doctor, encouraged me to do dilations as a means of expanding my practice and doing more to help my patients. With this push from my friend, I went back to my books, studied a little bit as a refresher, and then waited for a suitable patient to do my first dilation. It didn't take long. One day a seventy-nine-year-old man came in. Like many older people he had very small pupils. I didn't see any disease when I looked at his eyes, but because his pupils were so small, I felt I could do a better job if I made them bigger—that is, if I dilated. So, he became my first dilation patient.

I put the drops in his eyes, waited a half-hour until they took effect, and wow! His pupils went from three to eight millimetres. I was quite excited, though a little nervous, because now I was looking forward to doing a really complete exam. I looked into one eye and immediately understood that I could see much more by doing these dilations. It's a beautiful thing to be able to see inside the eye as it's the only part of the body through which you can see part of the central nervous system—the entire optic nerve. It's fascinating to view that, but it gave me a real jolt. In my original examination, when my patient was not dilated, everything had looked good. But now that his pupils were much bigger, I was able to see a cataract starting in his eye and little deposits, or lesions, on the retina of the eye. This was the beginning of macular degeneration. I could see the optic nerve very well and also noticed that it was a little bit larger in the middle—an indication of glaucoma. I referred the patient to an ophthalmologist, knowing that with an ordinary exam I probably wouldn't have. It was only when I had done the dilation and I could see much more that I felt a referral was necessary.

I felt I had done a good job. I felt excited, even exhilarated, to be doing more for my patients. That night when I came home, I got on the phone to my doctor friend so he could hear my excitement. I was thrilled with my first experience with dilation. It was a real revelation. It gave me a feeling of confidence and reawakened me to the beauty of my profession. It turned my practice around in many ways. It was literally an eye-opener.

Now I know I can do much more for my patients. Dilation is an important part of preventive medicine. Now when I see a patient who is highly myopic (very nearsighted), I know they are at risk for a detached retina or tears in the retina, so I know it's good to dilate to get a view of the whole retina. If a patient has cataracts, which is a film over the lens that obstructs vision, or glaucoma, a disease that damages the retina, I definitely want to dilate. A person who reports flashes or floaters in front of their eyes makes me want to see the retina, so I dilate, and I dilate anyone with macular degeneration or a family history of retinal problems. Diabetics are at risk for ocular complications, especially hemorrhages, so I also check the retinas of diabetic patients.

A lot of diseases of the eye don't have any symptoms. I often examine patients who are at risk for glaucoma, but they have no complaints—they see perfectly. As far as they're concerned, everything is fine, so it's important to get a good look at the optic nerve, and dilation is the best way to do that. You just never know. Sometimes I'm examining a very young patient, say a twenty-year-old, and I figure it'll be a breeze—there won't be any problems—but then I look into their eyes and see a cataract. A twenty-year-old kid with disease on the optic nerve. You can't take anything for granted.

Now that I'm doing dilations, there are other areas of optometry I'm thinking of expanding into. I think about working with children who have problems with the muscles of their eyes. They could be cross-eyed, for example. Not many optometrists delve into visual re-education, as it's called, where you help the patient use eye exercises to strengthen the muscles of the eyes so they won't be crossed. There's patching, where you patch the good eye to stimulate the bad eye to improve the vision. Or you can put drops in a patient's good eye to relax the vision of that eye, which is another way to force the bad eye to perform. That's another realm of optometry that interests me.

Dilations were a turning point. Doing them has made me a better optometrist, able to serve my patients better. And maybe I won't stop there.

One Surgeon, Two Lives

Jacob Langer

Photo by Dodge Baena

IT'S ABOUT A ONE-IN-A-HUNDRED-thousand long shot: twin babies who are born attached to each other. Conjoined twins. Separating them is often a delicate and complicated operation, and in some parts of the world it is impossible to even try.

But at Toronto's Hospital for Sick Children, they try. One of the pediatric surgeons there is Jacob Langer.

My father was a prominent surgeon, so I grew up with medicine around me. As a result, I thought the only reason I was interested in medicine was that my father was a doctor, so when I headed for university, I decided to do computer science. But after a fairly short period of time in that program, I realized I really did want to be a doctor. So, I switched out of computer science and went to medical school.

All through medical school I avoided surgery because, again, I thought the only reason to become a surgeon was that my father was a surgeon. Ultimately, I felt I had to decide between pediatrics and surgery, until one day it occurred to me that children needed surgery, too. So, I was able to combine my interest in children—I'd been a camp counsellor and a guitar teacher, and I'd always liked kids—with surgery, and I did my training in pediatric surgery.

Fast-forward to 2004, when I was the head of the division of general and thoracic surgery at SickKids. One day, I received an email from a woman named Rachel Spitzer. An obstetrics resident at the University of Toronto, she was at that time doing a three-month stint in Zimbabwe exploring her interest in HIV transmission from mother to child in the African context. She was also helping out in a clinic run by a Canadian doctor named Paul Thistle, who had married a Zimbabwean woman. Thistle had an ancient ultrasound machine, which he'd used one day on a woman who had walked a long way to get to his clinic, and discovered she was pregnant with conjoined twins. Rachel had helped Paul deliver the twins by Caesarean section, but it was clear to them there was no way to separate these babies in Zimbabwe. Yet it was also clear that, if they didn't get separated, they wouldn't survive. Unfortunately, this kind of thing happens quite often in the developing world—conjoined twins are born and can't be treated.

Rachel decided, "You know what? I know a hospital that can separate these twins."

Although I had seen Rachel once or twice, I really didn't know her, and she really didn't know me. Still, she emailed me a couple of pictures of the twins and an x-ray of them, and she asked, "Is there any way we can make this happen? Can we save them?"

I looked at the x-rays and the pictures and could see these baby boys were joined at the abdomen from just below their chests to just below their belly buttons. I could also see their pelvises were separated and their chests and hearts were separate, very important features in determining how difficult it would be to separate them. However, I couldn't tell how much of the liver was joined, whether their intestinal tracts were joined or whether their kidneys were normal. We'd have to bring them to Toronto to get a CT scan to figure those things out. But on the spectrum of conjoined twins, their situation was favourable, and I was confident we would have a good outcome for these boys.

Rachel also knew about the Herbie Fund, a program at SickKids Hospital that had been established in the late seventies. It's designed to pay for medical care for children from developing countries where they can't get a specific operation. The Herbie Fund pays for them to come to Toronto, for the treatment they need, and then go back to their country of origin.

After reading Rachel's email, I thought, this sounds like an appropriate case for the Herbie Fund and, fortunately, the fund agreed, so we had a start. But the Herbie Fund only pays for medical costs. It wouldn't pay for transportation to Canada or accommodations for the mother or her nurse, a woman who left her own family in Zimbabwe to come with the mom and stay with her the whole time. We had to raise money to cover those costs, and we did that by tapping contacts we had in the Jewish community.

The boys showed up in Canada in December. Tinashe and Tinotenda Mufuka were now four and a half months old, but it was clear to me they weren't ready for surgery. One, in particular, was pretty sickly because the blood flow between the two of them wasn't equal. One was getting more blood than the other, so we had to nourish them to get them ready for the surgery, and that wasn't easy because both had cleft lips and palates. A cleft lip is an opening in the upper lip, while a cleft palate happens when the roof of the mouth hasn't formed completely, leaving a space there. It can be repaired with modern surgery, and it's quite a simple operation, but until it was repaired, the twins would have trouble feeding. The whole process of applying suction to a bottle is something a baby with a cleft palate can't do, so initially we had to feed them through tubes right to their stomachs. Getting them to the point where they were strong enough to endure the separation surgery took another three months.

A couple of funny things happened during that time. The press found out about the twins and they became a very big item in the media. Coincidentally, my daughter got married just after the boys arrived in Canada. Just before the wedding there was a full-page story in the newspaper with a half-page picture of me, so we had all these out-of-town guests who had the newspaper dropped at the door of their hotel rooms with a big picture of me—it couldn't have been better timing. Then the day after the wedding, we left for a trip to Israel. We were sitting in the departure lounge at the airport and I could see people looking at their newspapers, looking at me, looking back at their papers, and trying to decide if that was me. It was quite funny.

As the twins got stronger, we began organizing the operational logistics. Separating conjoined twins is a team effort. It requires a general surgeon, of course, but it also requires plastic surgeons and anesthesiologists; depending on what organs are involved, it may require specialists in those areas, too; and it also requires nurses and the intensive care unit. You have to get everybody on board.

We performed the operation in March and it went well. It lasted about six hours, which isn't long for that kind of operation because it wasn't very complicated, and in terms of difficulty it was probably a seven out of ten. We divided the liver in half, which is technically challenging, but I've done many operations that were more technically challenging than this one. We had two slight complications or difficulties. One involved a technique called "tissue expansion." You implant what amounts to a plastic balloon under the skin and slowly fill it up with fluid. It stretches the skin over weeks and months so that when you close the abdomen—you can imagine when you divide twins there's a broad area to cover—it gives you extra skin to use. So, the plastic surgeon, Ron Zuker, put some tissue expanders in, but they got infected and we had to take them out. This was in the preparation stage before the actual separation.

When we did the separation, we were able to get one of the twins closed on the front, but we just didn't have enough muscle to do the other one, so we used a technique I have used for babies who are born with holes in their abdomen. We put a patch in the muscle that is designed to slowly dissolve and be replaced by the baby's own scar tissue, and that worked very well.

The operation and the process around it was a learning experience for our surgical trainees, nurses, social workers, anesthesiologists and critical care people. It taught all of them what goes into the separation of conjoined twins, which is a rare thing. Many of these people came from other countries and would eventually go back home, and my goal is always to teach them how to manage these kinds of cases themselves. For example, we've trained a lot of people from Saudi Arabia, where they have a very high incidence of conjoined twins. So now we rarely get conjoined twins from Saudi Arabia because they can take care of those cases themselves.

Tinashe and Tinotenda stayed in Toronto for a few more months so the plastic surgeon could repair their cleft lips and palates, and then they went home to Zimbabwe. They'd been here for about seven and a half months.

All these years later when people from SickKids go to Zimbabwe, they send back pictures and video clips of the boys. They are now teenagers who have the same quality of life as any other Zimbabwean boys. They are living proof of how we can make an enormous difference. We not only saved their lives, but we gave them excellent quality of life.

This is one of the special challenges of pediatric surgery. Any time you have a child's life in your hands, it's a profound responsibility because that child may have eighty years of living ahead. That's a long time if all we can provide is a questionable quality of life. And it's something that maybe you don't face when you're operating on an eighty-five-year-old.

People often say that surgeons are egotistical. I think that's true. But to me it's a good thing because if I didn't think I could take care of that baby at least as well as anyone else, how could I justify operating on him? If I believed in my heart that the guy down the hall could do it better, how could I justify doing it? I know some surgeons who don't have that confidence, and they struggle. Every time they go into an operating room, they're nervous and uptight. When I go into an operating room, I relax. I love the process. I love the intellectual challenge. I love the physical and technical challenge. I love the interactions with the families, too, because the vast majority of the time in pediatric surgery, things go well. The surgeon saves the child's life, or at least improves it. They fix the hernia, or make the pain stop, or fix whatever the problem is. They make the child better. That is an amazing feeling.

The worst situations I've experienced have been when I've lost a patient or had a poor outcome, and I think afterwards, I could have done better. But I have to make decisions in real time. I can be in the operating room at three o'clock in the morning and run into something unexpected. I can't say, "Let me go to the library to do some research and I'll get back to you." I have to make a decision on the spot. What am I going to do? And sometimes I think afterwards that the decision I made was not the best decision. When things go badly under those circumstances, it's really hard. I think that's why there's such a high level of burnout in surgeons. You have a lot of traumatic experiences that you never really deal with. It's slow torture, death by a thousand cuts. Eventually you hit a wall. It's happened to a lot of my colleagues. But for me, the few times that things have gone badly are balanced by the enormous number of times when things have gone well. That makes me love my work.

It was all good news with Tinashe and Tinotenda. One of them doesn't have a belly button and there are some scars, but other than that they seem like completely normal kids. And that is gratifying. I look back at the scrawny little kids with their cleft lips and palates who came to us as babies joined at the abdomen—two boys who almost certainly would have died had they not been separated. I see them now and they're just two teenagers playing with a soccer ball. Normal kids. That's hugely gratifying.

I See Very Determined Women

Erin Lurie

MOST OF US KNOW SOMETHING ABOUT drug addiction. Most of us also know something about pregnancy. But few of us think about the two conditions in one person. How do you deal with a drug addict who is pregnant? Even most doctors don't know the answer to that question.

Erin Lurie is one of the exceptions. She's a family doctor with a specialty in addictions and one of only four doctors in Ontario who deals with perinatal addiction. In theory, she devotes one afternoon a week to pregnant addicts, but she often finds herself working with this group of patients much longer than that. On the day we spoke she had just finished working five or six hours in the clinic on what was supposed to be a day off.

I'm often asked, "How many pregnant addicts are out there anyway?" I know we see about forty women a year in our clinic, but I can't give you an idea of what the numbers really are. There's so much stigma associated with drug addiction that pregnant women don't want to disclose their drug use to a doctor. The women I work with are often completely missed in the health care system. They often won't seek prenatal care because of their fear that social workers will take their babies away from them. Many in the health care field also malign them because they're seen as people with a moral weakness rather than as people with a recognized mental health diagnosis. I fell in love with perinatal addictions because I see very determined women. People with addictions are often trying to stop using substances or trying to make changes in their lives, and when a woman with an addiction becomes pregnant, it's a huge motivator for her to change.

In our clinic we often work with obstetricians who are very skilled in what they do, but just two days ago I spoke with an obstetrician who just wasn't able to recognize that his patient was in opiate withdrawal. If a doctor knows what to look for, the symptoms of withdrawal are obvious. Imagine the worst flu you've ever had and multiply that by one million. That's what withdrawal feels like. Your bones are aching. Your nose is running. You're sweating. You're vomiting. You have diarrhea. You feel terrible. But if a doctor doesn't know what to look for, these same symptoms can be mistaken for many other things.

In our clinic we work from a harm reduction model—that is, we try to reduce the harms from drug use. Today it might just be to get our patients to stop injecting drugs. Can you smoke them instead, which reduces risk? Or can you cut back on how much you're using? Can you stop sharing needles so you can avoid risks like hepatitis or

HIV? It can be a slow process. But as I said, patients often minimize their problem because they're so fearful that, if they tell you they're using drugs, you're going to call Children's Aid. As a result, many pregnant addicts don't seek prenatal care at all. They think that if they just show up when they're in labour, they can deliver their baby quietly and take her home.

There are two major issues when an addict who is pregnant isn't recognized and managed properly. The first is that a woman in opiate withdrawal can miscarry or go into labour early. So that's not safe. The second is the risks to the baby. There is no danger the baby will be born addicted to opiates because addiction implies a dependence on the drug or a craving for it, and that's not happening here. But the child has been exposed to the drugs in the uterus, and when he is born, he'll go through withdrawal. This is 100 per cent treatable if it is recognized. Baby will have no long-term consequence if he's treated properly. If it's missed or it's not treated properly, a baby can have seizures or die. With opiates, the problem is not exposure but withdrawal. I'm way more worried about babies who've been exposed to things like nicotine or cannabis or alcohol because those substances have long-term consequences from exposure alone.

I remember one pregnant patient, a woman in her thirties with an opiate addiction. She wasn't from the Toronto area, but she showed up in Toronto to get care. She had two kids she hadn't seen in years, and she really wanted to change, but she didn't know how to do it. She went to three hospitals before she connected with someone who was even willing to have a conversation about what to do for her. At that point she had already been in withdrawal for several days and was feeling terrible. So, after she had bounced from hospital to hospital and from doctor to doctor, someone finally called our clinic.

When she arrived, she was unstable and using substances. When I first see a woman like that, I think small picture: What can I do right now to stabilize things for her? What I often do is admit her to hospital because then she can see as many people as she needs to see. She can get ultrasounds and blood work. She can see a psychiatrist. She can get help with dental care, which she may never have had before. By hospitalizing her, I can get her the care that would normally take weeks and weeks to arrange for her as an outpatient. Then, when everything has settled a bit, I get to know who she is, what her life looks like, and how she pictures her life as it should be. There's so much mistrust of health care providers that these patients often won't disclose what they want right off the bat. In this case her other children had been taken away from her because of substance use, and she really wanted to parent the baby she was carrying.

We got her started on treatment, then followed her in her pregnancy. She ended up being quite stable on medication. She stopped using and came to all her appointments. She was getting all her prenatal care, and she went from feeling very lost in the system to very structured within it. We found her a place to stay during her pregnancy and a place where she could live after the baby was born. She had a boy, and everything continued to go amazingly well. She went into a supported living environment with her baby, and I saw her as she came in regularly for appointments.

One day last week, I was having a very challenging day. Things were not working out as I wanted. But then this same woman showed up at the clinic and she had her kids with her—all three of them—and she said, "It's been a year since I used anything." Not only that, it was also the first day in five years that she had seen her other children. She was planning to find a new place to live and start her life with her new kid, while re-establishing a relationship with her other children. She was in a really comfortable place. I sat there thinking about how many ways the system could have failed her by turning her away or saying, "You got yourself into this mess, so you figure a way out of it."

But we had got her the treatment she needed, and we had gone beyond medical treatment. We had put her in touch with a social worker and community outreach nurses. Now she has a whole new life ahead of her, which I think she would not have believed possible when she first came to hospital. It's cases like hers where I see I can really make a difference. In her previous pregnancies, nobody had given her the time of day. My kind of doctoring allowed her to have a happy outcome.

We're also slowly changing how others see these women. Plenty of doctors, I know, still think you can't change a drug addict. I sometimes get that eye roll when I talk about what I do or overhear a comment like, "What's the point?" But the nice thing at our hospital is that they've now seen the difference for a lot of these women. They've seen them come in and get stable and have positive results.

When I tell some of my friends what I do, they look at me and say, "That must be so sad." But it's actually the happiest part of my job.

Scared Healthy

Fred Saibil

Photo by Dahlia Katz

YOU HEAR IT SO OFTEN THAT IT'S become a cliché: the not-so-secret formula for maintaining good health is to watch your diet and exercise regularly. But it turns out you can use the same formula to regain your good health, even when you are very sick.

Fred Saibil is a gastroenterologist at Toronto's Sunnybrook Health Sciences Centre. He is a specialist in the treatment of inflammatory bowel disease (IBD), such as Crohn's disease and ulcerative colitis. He likes to help patients help themselves.

This is a story about a man I diagnosed with Crohn's disease when he was in his seventies. Crohn's can start at any age from infancy to extreme old age. It's a chronic disease of the digestive tract that can lead to abdominal pain, severe diarrhea, fatigue, weight loss and malnutrition. There is no cure, but we work to control it.

Let's call this patient Paul. His disease was mild for quite a few years, so I would only see him once a year. Then, when he was eighty-eight years old and he was at his cottage near Peterborough, east of Toronto, he got sick with his Crohn's and was admitted to the hospital there. They let me know he was there and told me what they were doing for him and it sounded okay.

After a few days the doctors there thought he was well enough to go home, so he went back to his cottage. But a few days later he called his kids and said, "I'm really sick. I'm vomiting. I think I'd better go back to Toronto." The kids went to pick him up—and they literally had to pick him up—and bring him to our hospital.

Paul had lost a lot of weight, and he was so weak that he couldn't sit up in bed on his own. He certainly couldn't walk or even stand, so he must have been having trouble with his Crohn's for a while. He was a tough, hard-nosed business guy, so in retrospect I think he had probably let things go for quite a while. He wasn't telling anyone that, when he was eating, he was bloating, or that he'd been restricting his diet to avoid the pain. But gradually his intestine was building up scar tissue and getting narrower and narrower until, practically speaking, it was blocked. He was sick because he had what we call a "high-grade small bowel obstruction." It wasn't going to get better without an operation, but he was far too weak to undergo surgery. He had to gain weight. He had to gain strength.

When people are as weak as Paul was, the immune system doesn't work well. Complications of surgery are more numerous, and healing is greatly impaired. There are also other postoperative complications such as blood clots in the legs or a pulmonary embolism, which can kill you. And a very weak person can't cough very well, increasing the risk of pneumonia after surgery. We had to reverse what was happening to his body strength. When you're eighty-eight years old, you lose your muscles easily. Some studies say you can lose up to 5 per cent of your muscle strength in a single day. This is especially true if there is some big inflammatory process going on in your body that is sucking the calories out of you.

So Paul was just lying around in the hospital. When I see anybody lying around, I go in and give them a speech. I say to them, "I have to ask you a tough question: Do you want to live, or do you want to die?"

I've had people in their nineties say, "I want to die. All my friends are dead. I've had enough."

I say, "Okay, then. I'll leave you alone."

But Paul said he wanted to live, so I told him, "That bed is the enemy. You are lying there doing nothing, and your muscles are getting weaker and weaker. If you sit up with your legs dangling down, you're already way ahead because you're using your back muscles to sit up. Use your muscles or lose your muscles." I wish every patient in the hospital could be given a broom so they could sweep the floor around their beds. Or maybe they could make their own beds. There's nothing to do when you're in the hospital, and as a result people do nothing and they get very weak.

Paul was a bright man, and he had a smart and committed family. When I have that situation, I tell the patient, "Listen, you have to help me help you get better. And your family is also going to help me to help you to get better." I try to make the patient and the family part of the treatment. Patients shouldn't feel like they're just bumps on a log, sitting there saying, "Help me."

So, I asked Paul, "How many people do you have in your family who are going to come to visit you? Tell them never to come at the same time. Make a schedule. Have them come one at a time." And I told the family, "You're not coming here to be entertained by your father. You're here to help me make your father better." Everyone agreed to work toward that.

For years I have been giving a set of exercises to people who are too weak to get out of bed or are just generally weak. It's a program of isometric exercises. I hold out three fingers and ask them to squeeze as hard as they can. I hold my hand up in front of them and tell them to push it away. I have them pull my hand toward them as well. I also have leg exercises. They're simple resistance exercises that can be done with every family member who visits. I have them do these exercises every hour they're awake. I have a missionary zeal about this program. I scare them out of bed, but it works—I get them up. Paul was the perfect patient. I didn't have to scare him because he was smart and committed and had no intention of dying.

He still couldn't eat, so I put him on a liquid diet that supplied all the proteins, carbs, fat, vitamins and minerals he needed. The diet doesn't supply enough water, so he could drink water-based fluids. I sent him home and he kept doing the exercises and stayed on that diet. His family kept working with him, and he gained back his strength and all the weight he had lost. He had surgery and sailed through it, and before too long he was back to normal. To me it was very gratifying working with him and with his family. I still remember how weak he was and how far he came. It was an extremely gratifying case for me.

A year later I opened a piece of mail and inside there was a note from Paul that said, "Thank you for everything." He also gave a generous donation in my honour to the Crohn's and Colitis Foundation, which is now called Crohn's and Colitis Canada, and he told them I saved his life.

There are a lot of times in medicine when you do save someone's life, but they don't realize it. You just know you did it, and that's your satisfaction. But when you get that feedback—when the patient knows you saved his life—it's very nice.

Small-Town Trauma

Mohamed-Iqbal Ravalia

IF YOU WERE TOLD THAT THE NEXT STORY was from a family doctor in Twillingate, Newfoundland and Labrador (population 2,196), you might reasonably conclude it would be a pretty sleepy story. But you would be wrong.

That's because Mohamed-Iqbal Ravalia, who became a Canadian senator in 2018, is not your typical small-town doctor.

I was born and raised in Rhodesia, which is now Zimbabwe. I did my medical training during a civil war, so a significant part of my training included dealing with trauma. I also undertook intensive training in anesthesia, emergency and obstetrics/gynecology, which kind of honed my skills for dealing with acute emergencies. In 1984 I immigrated to Canada and set up practice as a GP anesthetist in rural Newfoundland.

I have a very clear memory of a case from the late nineties. I was in a deep slumber at about two o'clock in the morning. I wasn't on call or working that day. The phone rang and I heard a rather panicked voice on the other end. It was a nurse named Vanessa who was working in the hospital emergency room that night. She said, "Ravs, I wonder if you could come down. We really need you. We have an acute emergency."

I got out of bed, jumped into my vehicle and made the short drive to the hospital, still rather sleepy. When I arrived in the emergency room, it was chaos. A young man was lying on the table with an obvious and horrendous wound to his neck area. I could see some red bubbly secretions in his neck area and I could sense panic all around me.

There was no time to ask questions then, but later I learned this man had been drinking and had either fallen asleep or fallen down at the side of the road where he had been struck in the neck area by a vehicle with a low-lying fender and partially decapitated. The extent of the trauma was dramatic. When I lifted his neck, I really didn't think he was going to make it.

In my training in Zimbabwe I had seen a lot of horrendous, nightmarish injuries. Over time I had become a little desensitized or conditioned to seeing trauma in its absolute worst form. But then I came to this place in rural Newfoundland where you never even see a gunshot wound, and now here in front of me was this horrendous trauma. I guess I had forgotten how difficult it could be. But the way I had been trained, and I think the way most doctors are trained, was to immediately get into save-the-life mode. So, I just jumped in. It was a reflex to do everything I could to save this young man's life.

I quickly ascertained that his airway was compromised and there was severe damage to his trachea. Somehow I had to get a tube down into his airway so we could get oxygen into his body and start resuscitating him. We cleaned the area, suctioning out debris and blood until we were able to introduce a small airway tube into the site where his trachea was punctured. Now we could see whether there were other significant injuries, and remarkably, there didn't seem to be any. We did blood work and took x-rays, which didn't really reveal anything more in terms of significant trauma. Incredibly, there was no injury to the spine or spinal cord, just this terrible injury to his neck and everything around it, including muscle, airway and blood vessels.

Once the young man's breathing was under control and his blood pressure was fine, he became agitated and needed sedation. By this time, we realized he had to be transferred to a bigger hospital where he would get the level of care he needed. This meant getting him to St. John's, which was a five-hour drive or a one-and-a-half to two-hour helicopter ride away. We contacted the Royal Canadian Air Force's Search and Rescue Squadron in Gander, and fortunately a Cormorant helicopter was available and could be in Twillingate in about an hour. While we waited, we continued tidying things up, making sure there was no active bleeding and patching his wounds as best we could. We made sure his tetanus status was up to date and gave him antibiotics—all the routine medical stuff. By now his temperature was down, he was calm and he seemed to be doing a whole lot better. Just before daybreak the search and rescue helicopter arrived, and we bundled the patient up for transport.

The Cormorant is a large chopper so there's lots of room to work. And the individuals on the chopper—myself, a nurse and a paramedic from Twillingate, and the regular search and rescue techs—had a great collection of skill sets on offer. We kept the patient sedated and maintained good blood pressure, so the transport was uneventful. When we arrived in St. John's and did the handover, they took him straight to the operating room.

We'd had some breakfast and were considering how to get home when the captain of the Cormorant came up to us and said, "We're flying back to Gander now, so we'll just take you aboard and drop you off in Twillingate. That will save you having to take a commercial flight home."

That sounded good to me, so we got on the helicopter. However, while we were flying over Terra Nova National Park, I heard a loud sound in the rear of the Cormorant, and before we knew it the captain had ditched us on a little sandy beach in the national park. Subsequently we learned there had been some recurring issue with the rear rotor, and there had to be all kinds of repairs done to the helicopter. Eventually we made it home.

Right after that adventure came a very reflective period for me—a deep, dark, melancholy period. It seemed I had experienced so much emotion and multiple life-and-death experiences over too short a period of time. I had some angst, some nightmares, some concerns about whether I had done all the right things. Had I resuscitated someone who was already near death, condemning him to a vegetative state? I got up in the middle of the night in a cold sweat, reliving the whole situation, hoping that I hadn't put him into further jeopardy. If he was going to survive but was significantly brain-damaged, had I made it worse for him and his family? All those kinds of thoughts went through my mind as I waited to hear the outcome.

Then over time I began to get notes back from the hospital in St. John's about what had happened in the operating room, the young man's recovery in the acute-care centre and his subsequent transfer to a restorative facility. I would run into his happy relatives who would give me feedback and say he was doing well. And, of course, I got busy with other stuff.

Then lo and behold, one day I was in the clinic when he walked in with his mother. He brought me a little gift and he had a broad smile. I didn't know who he was at first, but I recognized his mother and put two and two together. He looked so different from the alien and surreal body lying on the table that night that it was really unbelievable.

When I look back on my career, this was really one of the seminal moments. It was an instance when I had a huge effect on someone's life. This man had been lying near death right in front of me, and the procedures and resuscitation we instituted had made all the difference between life and death. The young man who walked into my office was fully functional. It was a very, very emotional moment—not just for the young man and his mother, but for me as well.

Seeing the Whole Patient

Ron Charach

Photo by Becca Gilgan

IT'S ALWAYS EASIER TO GO ALONG TO GET along, as the saying goes, and this is no less true for doctors than for the rest of us. But there are times when you just know in your heart that going along is not the right thing to do.

Ron Charach is a psychiatrist in outpatient practice. But like just about every doctor, he started his medical career working in a hospital. An early experience there has stayed with him and helped determine how he practises his specialty today.

When I was a psychiatry resident in a city on the prairies in the mid-seventies, I was on call in the emergency room when a very unruly woman, who seemed to be in her forties, was brought in. She was very drunk, dishevelled and verbally abusive towards the police and ER staff, so I'll call her Mrs. A. for "alcoholic" and "abusive." I learned that she had come in like this several times over the past few months and staff was sick of dealing with her—especially her foul-mouthed verbal attacks. There were no beds available in the alcohol treatment unit and a long waiting list to get in, so what to do with her?

There was something about the way Mrs. A. cut people up that seemed a bit grandiose at times, at least to me. She had a real flair for it—her insults could be very funny. With that in the back of my mind, I decided to stick my neck out a bit and admit her to the general psychiatry unit of the hospital rather than agreeing to discharge her. She would be admitted, whether she liked it or not.

This was a relatively rare plan of action. A psychiatrist's training is to try to talk a person into accepting an inpatient admission voluntarily. It is only when the person lacks insight and conveys the sense that, if discharged, they will cause harm to themselves or to someone else—in other words they pose an imminent threat—that psychiatrists typically resort to involuntary admission. Given the degree to which Mrs. A. was getting drunk and the growing intolerance of ER staff in dealing with her, my opinion was that it wasn't an option to let her keep going the way she was.

When you put somebody in a locked unit, however, there's another kind of risk involved. There may be dangerous people on the unit with whom the patient could interact in a bad way. So it's not something that's done lightly or cavalierly. The advantage to this course of action in this case was that, once Mrs. A. was an inpatient, she'd have no choice but to dry out. We could give her the pills she needed to help prevent seizures while she withdrew from alcohol, and I would be able to watch her over the course of several weeks.

Observing her turned out to be a very tall order. Mrs. A. kept breaking the rules. Whenever she was allowed out on a pass to see her family, she would come back late and sometimes very drunk. The nursing staff began pushing to discharge her. Meanwhile Mrs. A.'s marriage was in a shambles, family members were looking after her two children, and the family had largely given up on her. There wasn't much that was positive.

When we finally managed to get her to the point where she had gone a couple of weeks without anything to drink at all, Mrs. A. grew very depressed, slow thinking and slow moving. Then suddenly one day, in the space of a few minutes, she went from being extremely low to being extremely high, cracking jokes a mile a minute and being overly familiar with staff. In psychiatry we call this a "mood switch." She was looking frankly manic, something no one had ever observed in her before.

I started her on lithium, a classic treatment for manic depression, and over the next week or so she became more and more normal. She lost interest in getting drunk and experienced surprisingly few cravings for alcohol. She showed genuine insights into her past misbehaviour and all the suffering she had put her family through, and after a few weeks I was able to discharge her from the hospital. She continued with me in treatment as an outpatient, and in the months ahead she returned to family life and patched things up with her exhausted husband. Eventually she took a job with a sobriety organization, where she excelled enough to wind up holding an executive office—not a bad outcome!

It was only because I was a doctor that I was able to take charge of her deteriorating life situation against her will. Of course, this kind of power can be misused or abused, but sometimes taking control of someone's life can help save it from going down the tubes. Mrs. A. taught me a lot about "secondary alcoholism," or alcoholism that is a cover for some other serious underlying psychiatric disorder. In her case it was bipolar disorder with accompanying attention deficit disorder. She was using alcohol to get away from her mood swings and didn't even know she was doing it.

Early in my career, Mrs. A. forced me to recognize that each patient I deal with is a complex being with a mind, a brain, a personality. But that person also has a physical body to think about. For example, a particular patient's genetic predisposition and individual neurochemistry may be magnifying mood swings or disturbing patterns of thought. Social factors may also be involved, such as the way the person's family is responding to their challenging behaviour. Sometimes the family even plays a clear-cut role in contributing to that disturbing behaviour, such as in cases of physical or sexual abuse and other types of trauma.

I have learned to be a bit of a detective to see how all the parts interact to contribute to a problem. Everybody is a different puzzle. I get impatient these days when I hear some doctors talking about people as if they are just minds or brains, as if they didn't also have bodies, and when I hear other doctors who think a problem is all physical, that nothing social or psychological is going on. Such reductionism is not simply naive, but dangerous. All kinds of things are happening at the same time. To me, a doctor—and certainly a psychiatrist—should be able to meld together these different kinds of disparate factors and put them together to come up with a therapeutic plan.

An American internist and psychiatrist, George Engel, came up with ideas that later became known as the "biopsychosocial model," his prescription for making medicine more of a science. Yet, it seems like each and every doctor has to reinvent or rediscover this helpful wheel.

If I hadn't forced Mrs. A. into the hospital that night, who knows what would have happened to her? Instead, she turned her life around 180 degrees. If she could do that, I always ask myself, how many other mentally ill women and men can?

Where Everybody Knows You

Heather Morrison

AS CANADA'S SMALLEST PROVINCE, Prince Edward Island has a population of roughly 150,000 people. This means at least thirty-one Canadian *cities* have populations larger than that of this entire province.

Heather Morrison is the island's chief public health officer. Although this is a full-time job, she also works some nights and weekends as an emergency doctor at Charlottetown's Queen Elizabeth Hospital.

I got all my clinical training in Toronto. It was excellent training, but over the many years I was there not once did I see or treat a patient I knew or had a connection with. When I returned to PEI, one of the other physicians who was used to life on the island asked me, "How did you feel when you treated patients you knew in Toronto?" When I told him I hadn't treated anybody I knew in Toronto, he could not understand how that could happen.

Practising in Prince Edward Island is unique in ways like that. As a doctor here, I know that every day I go to work I am going to see people I'm familiar with. Whether it's my neighbour or a friend, or a friend of a friend, or a friend of my parents, or someone I knew when I went to school, or someone who knows my grandmother, I'm going to see people I know. And that reality makes for a different mindset.

I hadn't been back from Toronto very long when this hit home. One day a man I had known as a teacher when I went to school had a cardiac arrest. He came into Emergency, but we couldn't save him. He was only about fifty years old. His wife and children had heard he'd had a heart attack and rushed to the hospital, but by the time they arrived, he had died. When I walked into the room to see them their first questions were, "How is he? Is he going to be okay?"

I knew the truth would be devastating. Their husband and father had died, and they weren't even going to have the chance to say goodbye. It was tough. I remember it because it was the first time as a practising physician that I had to deliver this kind of news. It was the first time I did it by myself. And it was the first time it involved someone I had known. I get teary now when I think about it because it was such an emotional moment.

Of course, there have been multiple times since then when I've confronted difficult situations, such as having to tell someone my own age they have a tumour. Delivering bad news is not something doctors talk about very much. I guess I've learned how to tell people news that hurts. I've read about different approaches and techniques, but it's quite different having to do it relatively regularly in a community where I have close connections. I may see a person on a regular basis at the grocery store or kids' hockey games for years to come, and we'll always have that moment we shared. It never goes away. But since I know I'm going to be associated with that kind of devastating news, I've come to think of it in another way. I'm not an outside agent at these times. I'm inside. I'm *sharing* particularly challenging times with a family and a patient.

I think about these kinds of things in the setting of a community where I have lots of connections. It's made me realize how privileged I am to share those moments of sorrow and sometimes hope—the privilege of sharing a human connection. It's these moments that make me realize I'm doing something important. I would never have been able to articulate that before going into medicine. There's an actual ache I feel in someone's distress or while giving them bad news that impacts me all the time. I have empathy and concern for these patients. And looking at it from the other side, I also hope that perhaps hearing unwanted news from someone they know may provide a slight comfort and reassurance.

When I started in medicine, I may have thought of it as something really exciting and romantic. Now I think I understand that the reward of being a physician, especially in a smaller community, is being so connected to other people. I have been humbled by the love that I witness between patients and their families. Sometimes in the hospital I'll walk by a room and glance in. I'll see an elderly patient lying in the bed and there beside him, for hours or even days on end, is his spouse. Sometimes that person is giving him a drink of water or washing his face. That's real love and caring and I get to see that on a regular basis.

I'm sometimes so impressed that families and patients are so gracious. I got teary with a family recently because of the way they were talking about a family member who was very ill. The way they spoke about this loved one really showed how much they cared and respected his wishes. I walked away feeling lucky to be able to see the love and support in that room. I went home thinking, wow, that was amazing!

This can be a hard profession, but it can also be a wonderful, humbling profession. I feel especially privileged to be able to practise in a community where I care about the people and I have a bond with so many of them.

Knowing Everything about Almost Nothing

Duncan Anderson

OUT OF ABOUT EIGHTY-SEVEN thousand doctors in Canada, only a handful are neuro-ophthalmologists. They are subspecialists of both neurology and ophthalmology, trained in the diagnosis and treatment of visual problems related to the brain rather than the eye.

Duncan Anderson is one of this rare breed. He works at three British Columbia locations—St. Paul's Hospital and two sites of Vancouver Hospital and Health Sciences Centre (formerly known as Vancouver General Hospital and UBC Hospital).

The eyes are the most important connection to the brain. In fact, there are more nerve fibres going to the brain from the eyes than from anywhere else in the whole body. The average neurologist knows the brain but doesn't really understand the eyes very well. And the average ophthalmologist knows the eyes but doesn't know much about the brain. They're two totally different training programs.

My specialty combines the two, so I have a unique practice. The cases that come to me are the ones based on very obscure visual complaints and symptoms. It's not just that the patient has blurred vision because she's got a cataract. The cases I see are those where the two specialties, neurology and ophthalmology, can't figure it out unless they put their heads together.

Ninety per cent of my referrals come from neurologists. They say, "I don't know what's going on in this patient's brain. He is not well, and he complains about his eyes, and I can't figure it out." The other referrals come from ophthalmologists. They say, "This patient is losing vision. I've done all the tests. He doesn't have cataracts. He doesn't have glaucoma. But he's losing his vision, and I haven't got an answer." By the time the patient sees me, he's already seen one or two neurologists who can't figure it out, one or two ophthalmologists who can't figure it out, and maybe a neurosurgeon or two. These patients have sometimes been hunting for a solution to their problem for years. Despite visiting doctor after doctor, they are still suffering. So, the buck stops with me. Of course, 99.9 per cent of the time the neurologists and ophthalmologists are able to come to a diagnosis, and they're going to be right. It's that last .1 per cent that I get, the cases where all the tests have been done and no one has been able to diagnose the problem.

I got very good training as a neuro-ophthalmologist at Harvard, but I always tell my residents that at the end of medical school and at the end of residency you know nothing. You just know how to learn. You learn how to become a very good doctor through experience, and that's the edge I have.

I'm seventy-six years old and learning every day. I've seen two or three thousand patients with complicated problems that most doctors won't see in their lifetimes. I have learned from each case, which is exciting to me. Some of these cases are very rare, maybe one in a million. It's the experience of having seen each obscure case that helps me figure the next case out. I sometimes read in a journal that there have been only three reported cases of this or that problem, but I've probably seen five just like them and not bothered to report them.

Every single patient is like a Sherlock Holmes mystery. I look at signs. I listen to how the patient talks and study how she looks. The complication in medicine is that patients aren't trained to explain exactly what's going on. They may not be articulate enough or a doctor may never have asked the right question in the right way to elicit the right information from them. Because I've seen so many patients, I have become very good at talking to people about obscure symptoms, figuring out what they're trying to tell me, figuring out what tests to do and how to fix whatever is wrong.

The most common diagnosis for unexplained visual loss is a slow-growing meningioma—a tumour in the head. It's benign—it's not going to kill you—but it grows in the space right around the eye so it can cause double vision or progressive loss of vision. In routine scanning these tumours are hard to find because they are very small and grow in obscure places. Ordinarily a neurologist with a patient who has unexplained visual loss orders a CT scan of the entire head, but doesn't direct the radiologist to focus on a particular area. Once I suspect meningioma, I tell the radiologist, "I want you to scan this area, this exact spot of the visual cortex of the brain." And then they find it. If I go back and look at perhaps three CT scans or three MRIs over the last ten years for the same patient, I will see that the tumour was always there, but the tests were all read as normal because the radiologist hadn't been told where to focus. Now we can do neurosurgery, take out the tumour, and then after ten years of progressive visual loss it stops. Very often the patient returns to normal. So, it's not that I'm always coming up with a rare diagnosis. Sometimes it's just a matter of having the experience to put all the evidence together and realize that the doctors before me were barking up the wrong tree.

Other times, there really is no answer. All the neurologists and ophthalmologists haven't been able to figure out the disease because there is no physical disease. But there might be a psychological disease. Perhaps the patient is terribly worried about something. When I tell the patient what I've found, they often say, "Twenty doctors told me I probably have a brain tumour and you're telling me I don't." They may not be happy because they prefer the idea of a physical illness. They don't want someone to tell them they have a psychological problem. Sometimes they become very angry, though that's a small minority of patients. The vast majority say something like, "I wish I'd seen you five years ago or ten or twenty years ago. Every doctor just sent me home with painkillers or whatever, but you listened to me, and then you did some tests that I hadn't had before, and you found the problem." They are really, really happy, which obviously makes me happy.

I always knew that medicine could be boring, at least for me. I didn't want to do coughs and colds. Even cataract surgery gets repetitive after you've done it three thousand times. But people are the most interesting things in the world. What has kept me going, kept me feeling young, and kept me thinking and learning is dealing with people with strange complaints that I could figure out. That has been endlessly fascinating.

The young doctors I train today think I'm brilliant. I'm not. I'm just very good in a very narrow specialty. I tell them what my daughter always says. She's a GP. She says, "Dad, I know nothing about almost everything. You know everything about almost nothing."

Doing the
Right Thing

Neill Iscoe

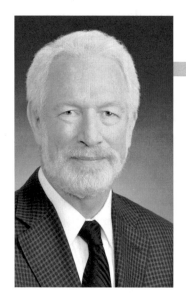

FOR ALL THE ADVANCES MADE IN treating cancer, the C-word still has the capacity to strike fear into us. And rightly so. The Canadian Cancer Society says half of us will develop cancer in our lifetimes, and a quarter of us will die from it. More than 200,000 cases are diagnosed every year.

Neill Iscoe is an oncologist at the Odette Cancer Centre, part of Sunnybrook Health Sciences Centre in Toronto. He's learned that, although not every patient can be saved, every patient can be helped.

I guess I should start with a spoiler alert: the story I'm going to tell is about one of my proudest moments as a doctor, but the patient dies in the end. That may sound odd, but the special part of this story is that so many people came together to help this patient and never lost sight of what was really important.

The man—I'll call him James—was admitted to hospital with melanoma. Most people hear that word and think of skin cancer that starts in basal cells. That's the most common kind, and it only rarely does serious damage. This patient had a much more serious type of melanoma, and this was the mid-eighties, a time when treatments for a spreading melanoma weren't worth a damn.

I don't remember if I'd seen him before he was admitted, but I was the guy taking care of melanoma patients, so I was looking after him, and I knew he was going to die very soon.

He was young—in his mid-thirties. His marriage had failed. His wife, apparently a drug user, had disappeared from his life, but she was the mother of his two kids. I think they were twins about six or eight years old. One of them had caught measles at some point and become deaf as a result.

James had been in the midst of making out his will and working out who would take care of the children after he died. He thought his wife wasn't capable, so he wanted to appoint a trusted family member as their guardian. He hadn't yet completed his will when he had a stroke. The melanoma had spread to his brain and he was comatose—completely unresponsive.

When this happens, it usually leads to a discussion with the family about resuscitation. But if the patient is going to die, I tell them it is a question of how many times they want to look into the abyss. For some people, patients and families, resuscitation offers a chance to say a goodbye—a chance they would not otherwise have.

This assumes the medical team believes resuscitation is likely to result in a level of consciousness that will allow useful interactions, which is clearly a judgment call. Those who have already said their goodbyes may find resuscitation inappropriate.

In this case we knew that James had been desperate to finish writing his will. I had two young boys at the time, and I was acutely aware that I wouldn't have wanted them to fall into harm's way because I hadn't finished doing something that would have protected them. If James didn't complete his will, the kids might go to his ex-wife by default because that's what the law would have required. Someone might have been able to start a legal process to stop it, but it could have been a long process, and maybe it wouldn't have succeeded. In the meantime, no one knew what the kids might have to go through.

So, we worked to resuscitate him, using medication to temporarily decrease the swelling around his brain. It worked—James became alert again. The social worker and I immediately began putting things in place so he could complete his will. We knew we had to work fast.

James was not able to speak because of where the melanoma was, but because one of his children was deaf, he had learned how to sign. The social worker—and this is a great tribute to her—approached the Bob Rumball Centre for the Deaf, which fortunately is just up the street from the hospital. Bob Rumball himself came over and communicated with James through sign language.

We also knew that for legal purposes somebody had to establish that James was mentally competent when he completed the will. I called the psychiatrist who generally worked with the cancer program and said, "I've got a problem. This is a real problem. You need to get here this afternoon." The psychiatrist came by, asked James some questions through the deaf interpreter, and was satisfied of his mental stability.

Then the lawyer who had been working on the will came. He had a nice, typed, five-page uncompleted will. He assessed the situation, ripped up everything he had, and as I recall, wrote down twelve or fourteen points and got James's signature on it. This all happened within three or four hours, which was unheard of. James died within a week.

This story is not so much about medicine, or what we usually think of as medicine. It has to do with common sense and doing what was right for James and his family—doing what he would have wanted.

Any time somebody is told "We don't have any more treatment that is going to be worthwhile for you," when they're told "It's not a matter of if, but when," it's always too quick. But many patients use that as an opportunity to think of those they'll leave behind, which is really heroic. James was an example, one of those people who does heroic things in a terrible situation. One of those people who think beyond themselves. Being a doctor sometimes allows me to meet those people and support them in their last, heroic act.

The Girl in the Yellow Dress

Andrew Furey

Photo by David Howells

AFTER YEARS OF SPECIALIZED TRAINING, doctors possess important and valuable skills. Many find it incumbent upon themselves to use these skills to help people in faraway places where medical care is either rudimentary or nonexistent.

Andrew Furey is one of those doctors—an orthopedic surgeon from St. John's who uses his skills and talents around the world.

I'm an orthopedic surgeon and I did specialty training in ortho- pedic trauma—broken bones. In January 2010 I had only been practising for about three years and a bit when a terrible earthquake struck in Haiti. Hundreds of thousands of people were killed, and hundreds of thousands more were injured. I saw all the images of the destruction and the suffering on the television in my living room, and it was immediately evident to me that people would be dying from head injuries or abdominal injuries, but they weren't neces- sarily going to die from their broken bones. It was obvious, too, that these thousands of people with broken bones would need care, and they would be a tremendous burden not only to themselves and their families but to the whole medical system in the wake of a nat- ural disaster like this. So I said, "Okay, this is what I do for a living. I fix broken bones. That's my bag of tricks. We'll see how I can help."

I had just returned to Canada from Baltimore, where I had done fairly intensive trauma training, so I knew the University of Maryland had people on the ground in Haiti before the earthquake doing HIV research. Because of the geographic proximity and frankly because of the horrendous burden of that disease in Haiti, it was the right place to send people to study, but after the earthquake it didn't make any sense to study HIV there. What the people of Haiti needed at that time was a trauma centre, and the university quickly switched its research outfit to a trauma provider outfit. I volun- teered with them.

I went to Haiti several months after the earthquake to put my surgical skills to use. We operated in a partially collapsed building and the patient wards were intense. I remember one man who was transferred to us on our second or third day in the country. His hip had been fractured in the earthquake, and he had been lying in a medical tent for months, waiting for someone with the capacity or capability to fix it. This wasn't all that unusual, given the number of muscular skeletal injuries the earthquake had caused.

But while I remember him well, I remember the person with him even better—his caring companion, his support, his loved one. She was his twelve-year-old granddaughter, a little girl in a yellow dress with braids in her hair. Her parents had been killed in the earthquake, so she was an orphan. She sat with her grandfather before the operation, she walked with him to the operating room, and then she went outside to wait under some trees for the operation to be over.

As I said, the grandfather had a broken hip, so we replaced it. Without this operation his future would have been grim. As he had no money, he might never have received medical care, and he would literally have lain in a hospital bed for the rest of his life. That was his future. When I came out of the operating room, I took off my surgical mask and walked over to the granddaughter, still sitting outside waiting for news. I told her the surgery went okay. She reached out and shook my hand, showing maturity well beyond her years. She was just twelve years old! She should have been in grade 6 or 7 learning to read and write. She should have been playing with Barbies, but instead she was orphaned and looking after her grandfather.

The look in her eyes has never left me. It told me that not only had I given a gift to the grandfather, I had given an incredible gift to her. Our whole team had given an incredible gift to her. Hip replacement is a really common surgery in orthopedics, and it only took maybe twenty to forty minutes, but that look in her eyes made me understand that I had changed and maybe even saved her life by giving her back her grandfather. It's a moment I have carried with me for my entire surgical career.

I was so deeply affected by the Haiti experience that I created our own Canadian medical volunteer force, and about ten months after I got home, I went back with two other doctors. It was supposed to be a one-time thing—Newfoundland and Labrador's contribution to Haiti's recovery effort—but it very quickly took on a life of its own. We hadn't been back home for ten minutes after that second trip before everybody said they wanted to go again. So we started sending regular teams from Newfoundland and Labrador two or three times a year. From that, word spread across the country really quickly. Calgary heard about it and they said, "We can do that." Halifax heard about it and they said, "We can do that."

So we went from sending doctors to one location to nine locations, and from three volunteers to twelve hundred volunteers. It's now called Team Broken Earth. Initially it was only providing medical care and education in Haiti, but we've since expanded to other countries—among them Bangladesh, Ethiopia, Guatemala and Nicaragua. I go three or four times a year for a week each time, and it's a real eye-opener. It's sad and disturbing that so many people don't have access to medical care. And sometimes it's just overwhelming. We've seen young people die right in front of us who would not die in Canada. For example, often there's no access to blood products. There was one patient in particular I remember who bled out on the table. She was so young and her heart was so strong, but at the end of the day you could just see the clear saline being pumped through her arteries. Her body didn't want to give up the fight but there was just no blood. She'd been shot, and if she had been shot in Canada through an artery, we would have had enough blood to get her through the surgery, and she could have gone on to live a productive life. But not in her country, and that is a kick in the gut. That took the wind out of everybody's sails.

But you rebound. The team rebounds together. And we all feel an overwhelming sense of gratitude that we live in Canada and won't have to face that scenario. It's made all of us appreciate what we have at home. We can—and should—complain about how our health care dollars are spent in Canada, but at the end of the day it's not the burden we all think it is. We're all very, very, very lucky.

I'd love to change the system in Haiti or Bangladesh or wherever, but that's too big to take on. Somebody once said, "I'm not going there to change the world. I'm going there to change somebody's world." The team and the individuals on the team get a great deal of energy and at times solace from that. It's a reminder of how incredibly important it is to change one person's life. And it all started from that one episode, that one twelve-year-old girl who really touched me. To be honest, I didn't know at the time that she would have the impact on me that she did. I recognized something at the time, but the degree to which she would influence my future? I couldn't have predicted that. It was only weeks and months later when people started asking me about my experience, and I began to digest it all, that I said, "Wow! That was a pretty special moment." All these years later, prompted by nothing in particular, her face will pop into my mind. I'll see her yellow dress and the braids in her hair. There was a language barrier between us, but that look! I could really see in her eyes the gratitude and the hope that things could now get a little bit better.

I can tell all kinds of gruesome trauma stories from my career. Stories where I thought someone would never walk again, but they do walk, or stories about rebuilding the leg of a patient who was struck by a car and left on the side of the road. But there was something life-changing and poetic about that particular girl and that particular moment in time that has really stuck with me.

Eleven Minutes

Photo by Sarah Vandusen

Joshua Bezanson

IN A MEDICAL EMERGENCY, TIME IS NOT anyone's friend. It moves relentlessly, almost always worsening the prospects for the patient in distress. But dealing with a life-threatening crisis with one eye on the clock is an occupational hazard for many doctors.

Joshua Bezanson is a senior resident in emergency medicine and an EMS Fellow at the University of Alberta Hospital in Edmonton. He's a young doctor who has already felt the pressure of having to do the right thing at the right time.

I was working in one of the rural hospitals in small-town Alberta. It was a tiny hospital—twelve beds, maybe four or five nurses and a handful of nonmedical support staff.

One day a man in his early fifties came in. He had driven himself to the hospital because that's what you do in rural Alberta—you don't wait for an ambulance. He looked terrible. He was sweaty and vomiting. He said he had been feeling well, and then suddenly he felt a terrible, crushing chest pain. He said, "I was working at my desk half an hour ago, and this wave of sickness just came over me."

We brought him right in and started assessing him. In pretty quick order we were able to determine that his problem probably had to do with his heart. He was most likely having a heart attack. We hooked him up to have an electrocardiogram (ECG), and sure enough he was having a massive heart attack, what we call a "STEMI heart attack," which is the most serious type. It means there's been a total blockage of the coronary artery, starving the heart of oxygen, and this in turn can cause extensive damage to a large part of the heart. It's often called the "widow-maker" as the mortality rate for people who have this kind of heart attack is almost 50 per cent in the first hour.

We were in a pretty remote facility, far from one of the large centres with a cardiac care unit, but we were able to mobilize all the resources we had. I mean literally all the resources, not just the nurses and the people you would expect, as we had to do a lot of really time-dependent things. The lady in the cafeteria helped contact the man's wife. The housekeeper brought in clean sheets and got ready to help with CPR if we had to do it. Literally everybody in the facility stopped what they were doing and came to help this one sick man. My role was to lead the team.

Somebody who comes into a hospital with such terrible symptoms—a large blockage of the main artery that feeds the heart—really has only one hope of survival: getting rid of the blockage. To do that, we use powerful clot-busting drugs called "thrombolytics." They're sort of like liquid Drano—you inject the drug and it breaks up all the clots in the body. But it comes with some risk, the biggest of which is major bleeding. If the bleeding is in the brain, the patient has a stroke. It can be a tricky decision for a physician to order this medication. The last thing any doctor wants to do is make things worse.

The nurse was standing there with a syringe and asking, "Should I push it or not? You tell me."

You have to tolerate uncertainty and ambiguity in medicine. A staff physician was on his way to the hospital and talking to us by phone, but he couldn't see the patient. It was up to me and based on all the information I had in that imperfect setting, I thought there was more benefit to the drug than potential harm. We gave him the drug.

The neat thing is that when this drug works, it works really well. You can see the heart attack resolving in front of your eyes, on the ECG, and you say to yourself, "I feel better, too."

And we had good reason to feel better. We were able to get him onto the table, diagnose him, get an IV started, control his pain with morphine, give him some Aspirin, and get him the thrombolytic medication—all in eleven minutes.

There are published guidelines to aim for in these situations, and it's on the order of thirty to sixty minutes to do what we did in eleven minutes. This small, under-resourced facility in rural Alberta managed to give state-of-the-art care and beat all the benchmarks at the same time. I don't think even the bigger centres could compete with what we did. In spite of all the challenges of rural medicine, this was a time when everything clicked. And it was purely because of teamwork.

There's a special feeling in a small hospital. People know each other. Everything is personal. Chances are that somebody in the building knows the patient personally or knows the family of that person. Everything seems to have a sense of urgency that sometimes is lost in a big centre, where a patient might feel like a cog in a machine. Our whole team came together, and as team leader, I helped facilitate that. So, I was definitely feeling good. Even the cardiologists in Calgary, where we sent the patient, congratulated us on the job we had done.

But it only really hit home a few weeks later. After the patient was discharged and back home, he wrote a letter to the editor of the local newspaper. They published it with the headline, "Teamwork at Hospital Like Nothing I've Seen Before."

> *Recently I discovered just how lucky we are to have a first class hospital here and first class health care professionals.*
>
> *On May 23 I went to the hospital with what I recognized were heart attack symptoms and literally within seconds was being attended to by a multi-disciplinary group.*
>
> *Though my memory of that first fifteen minutes is a bit fuzzy, for the next hour I was fully alert and every minute will be forever embedded in my memory.*
>
> *They showed me the meaning of teamwork. Each person in that room knew exactly what they needed to do. I witnessed a rare display of human communication that I had never before experienced.*
>
> *The direction to and feedback from each team member was remarkable and gave me an amazing sense that I was in capable hands and would be just fine.*

Emergency medicine is the ultimate team sport, and the patient had picked up on the fact that this whole team had come together to take care of him. As a doctor, it was the first time I felt

I'd definitely made a difference in somebody's outcome, a tangible difference in a patient's life.

At the time I was finishing my internship, and it was just a few months before my residency started. I was literally in the last weeks of deciding what program I wanted to be part of. I could have done rural family medicine. I could have done lots of different things. But this event clinched it for me. I definitely wanted to go down the path of emergency medicine. That was the part of medicine that really excited me. You make decisions on the fly. You bring everybody in. You listen to everybody's opinion. There are so many different areas of expertise that people bring to a team. The team leader doesn't have to know it all, but he has to be the best communicator in the room. And that's what I enjoy. I enjoy the technical parts of medicine and the science parts of medicine, but what really excites me is the ability to bring order to chaos.

The Evil Eye

Daniel Carucci

THERE IS A LONG HISTORY OF PEOPLE from the developed world travelling to developing countries to bring modern advancements—new technologies, new medicines or sometimes new scientific information—to improve living conditions.

Daniel Carucci is a general practitioner who also has advanced degrees in clinical tropical medicine and molecular biology. He has spent most of his career fighting disease outside the developed world.

I had every intention of becoming an internal medicine physician, but after medical school I joined the US Navy. I intended to stay in for four years, but I stayed for twenty. I became a flight surgeon and learned to fly airplanes. I spent a lot of time in the tropics, led the Navy's malaria vaccine program, then left the navy and ran a program called the Grand Challenges in Global Health Initiative for the Bill and Melinda Gates Foundation. This program was set up to find innovative ways to solve difficult problems like poor nutrition, insect-transmitted disease and uncontrolled infections. Then I worked on issues of global health for the United Nations Foundation.

I eventually found my way to a health care communications company called McCann Health, part of the McCann Worldgroup, the largest marketing and advertising company in the world. They were interested in working with the United Nations, so I helped set up McCann's global health program. Which leads me to the story I'm going to tell.

A few years ago, I was on an assignment in Afghanistan funded by UNICEF. I was there to help their ministry of public health find more effective health communications strategies. Afghanistan gets many billions of dollars a year from various sources, but they weren't meeting their health targets. Naturally there was concern about putting even more money into services that people weren't picking up. There was a lot of supply in medical programs but not much demand, which is a reversal of the way things usually are.

While I was there, I noticed that all the young infants had little black threads tied around their wrists. It turns out this black thread is one of the first gifts the grandmother gives to the child at birth. But sometimes there was a little bead on the thread, so it looked like a tiny bracelet. I learned this bead was a *nazar*, which is meant to ward off the evil eye. Many cultures around the world believe that a particular glare can curse a person with evil spirits and cause serious bad luck. The bead is supposed to provide protection to the little child. It's a very powerful custom in that culture.

That custom triggered an epiphany or "aha moment"—something very magical—for me. I realized we could use the bracelets for protection, too, though not by keeping evil spirits away. We could use them as a way of indicating the child was protected against disease, a way of showing the child had been vaccinated. Afghanistan has the world's highest infant mortality rate. It's not just because children aren't being immunized, of course, but that's part of it.

With that insight, we created what we called the "immunity charm," a bracelet given to the mom when she first brought her child in for an immunization. Every time the mother brought the child in for another immunization, we would give her a different-coloured bead to represent the specific vaccine we'd given: orange for polio, purple for measles, yellow for hepatitis. Adding each bead to the bracelet meant the child was wearing an immunization record. The bracelet harnesses that record to a long-standing cultural belief that associates the beads with protection and provides a visible symbol of the mom's love and protection for her child. We hoped that when other moms saw it, they would want the bracelet for their child.

When we did an initial qualitative study in Afghanistan, we found the mothers loved the immunity charm. This provided anecdotal evidence that it was effective. But in order for us to scale up the program we needed hard data—we needed to prove this was actually increasing immunization coverage. We needed a study and it had to be done rigorously.

That study is happening now in India. We've identified several districts where we'll be deploying the immunity charm into the system, and we'll compare the changes in immunization rates over the course of twelve months to other districts that have not introduced the immunity charm. Once we have the data, and assuming it shows increased vaccinations, I think the floodgates will open, because then organizations like UNICEF and the World Health Organization will step in. An intervention that is so cost-effective and culturally relevant will be taken up widely.

The evil eye phenomenon is most strongly focused in South Asia, but it's been part of many cultures going back thousands of years. We have had some very preliminary discussions with countries in Africa where we think the immunity charm could become a social norm. But even if it's not part of a traditional belief system, it could catch on just because mothers like having these colourful bracelets for their kids. We have to see if that happens or not, but we think it could happen quite easily. There is already the infrastructure to make these bracelets available, and they're not an expensive intervention.

If this works to increase vaccine compliance, it could lead to significant progress against a big problem. More than three million people die from vaccine-preventable diseases every year, and about half of those deaths—about a million and a half—are children less than five years old. That's a lot of children who would not die if they were fully immunized.

I know this could not have happened if I hadn't been a physician. It couldn't have happened if I didn't have an appreciation of the importance of vaccines from my work running the navy's malaria vaccine program. It could not have happened if I had not worked in large-scale UN-type programs where I could see the impact of small, cost-effective interventions. And it could not have happened if I had not been working with a large medical communications company.

In life, we have many opportunities to reflect on what we have done. Maybe having this insight into the evil eye is satisfying to me because it's recent. But I also think that at some point the immunity charm is going to be one of the most powerful and talked-about interventions to reduce childhood mortality in the world.

From Patient to Doctor

Laura Tate

Photo by Michael Cooper

IT IS SAID THAT DOCTORS MAKE THE worst patients. That's supposedly because they know too much and can't stop second-guessing the physician who is looking after them. On the other hand, it may be that patients make the best doctors. It's certainly what Laura Tate has come to believe.

Tate is now a plastic and reconstructive surgeon at Michael Garron Hospital in Toronto, but when she was a child, she spent a long time as a patient in a hospital. What she learned about medicine while lying in bed informs her practice today.

I didn't even know my back was crooked, but at my grade 8 graduation we were taking pictures, and my mom said, "Would you stand up straight?"

I said, "I am standing up straight."

She said, "No, you're not."

I moved around a bit, but I still wasn't standing straight. No matter what I did, one shoulder was higher than the other.

I had scoliosis, which is an abnormal curvature of the spine. This was in the seventies, and at that time the surgery for straightening it involved stretching the spine and hooking rods into it, and then lying in a hospital bed for three months waiting for everything to set. For the first two weeks I couldn't move around at all, just lie there flat on the bed. I couldn't even sit up to eat.

I was twelve years old and on an adult floor, so there wasn't much stimulation except watching TV—the same game shows every day. There wasn't very much for my doctor to do after the surgery. It was just a matter of waiting, but he came to visit me every day. He didn't need to come, but he would pop in to see me. I also found out what a hard job it is to be a nurse. They were always after me to go down to the activity room, but I didn't want to go because I was embarrassed to be seen in the bed. For a long time I didn't go. Then one day the nurse said, "You're going." They wheeled me down to the room, and I had the greatest time. I did some basket weaving and some other things, and after that I was eager to go down there. That nurse was smart to push me when I didn't want to go.

I was always thankful for what the doctors and nurses did for me in that hospital, and I began to think I would like to be able to help people one day myself. That's why I became a doctor and having had experience as a patient has made me a better doctor. However, it wasn't easy at the beginning.

I can tell you a funny story. I had just finished medical school, and I was doing the plastic surgery rotation. I was so keen to make a good impression. One day they said to me, "We have a patient who needs a mole removed. Would you like to do it?"

I had watched doctors removing moles, so I said, "Sure."

I was put in this little room with the patient. No windows, just a door. There was no nurse—just the two of us. I looked at the mole. I put the freezing in. I got the tray of instruments ready.

I made the little cut and removed the mole. Then I realized it was bleeding. What was I going to do? I really hadn't thought that part out. I thought, oh, my gosh, there's nobody here. I put some gauze on it and tried to keep some pressure on it, all the while thinking: This is really not good. I don't want to call out for help. I don't want to look like I don't know what I'm doing.

All this stuff was going on in my head while I was looking around, trying to be calm. I decided to have a look under the gauze to see how much bleeding there was, and it had stopped! It was such a relief. Everything had gone well after all. I was so happy. I hadn't panicked. And I told myself: I am going to be able to do this. I'm going to be okay.

So those were the two learning experiences that made it possible for me to become the doctor I am today. Which means I can really use my skills to help people.

I remember a very special case early in my career. I met a man in intensive care who had meningococcal pneumonia. It was very serious. He was in shock and required a lot of medication to keep blood supplied to his heart and internal organs, but at the same time circulation was being stolen from his arms and legs. It was pretty horrendous. I had never seen anything like that before. His toes and fingers were blue, and eventually his toes mummified—the big toe dried up to look like a scab with a nail on it. The surgeons had to amputate both his feet, and though we tried to save as much of his hands as possible, I had to amputate parts of his fingers and thumbs. It was a miracle he survived.

As he slowly recovered, I met with him and his wife, and I was really impressed with his attitude because it was so positive. But after many, many outpatient visits I saw he was still having problems with the use of his thumbs. As there wasn't much there, he couldn't grip anything, and his fingers had been cut short so he couldn't make a fist to hold onto things. And since about 50 per cent of your hand function relies on your thumbs, he couldn't do some of the basic things of life, like pulling up his underwear or putting on his socks.

Normally, to lengthen the thumb, we would transplant the big toe to the thumb, but he didn't have his toes anymore, so that was out. I had read in my plastic surgery literature about an operation that could make the space between the thumb and the index finger a little bit deeper, which would have the effect of making the thumb longer. But I had never done that operation and I didn't know anybody else who had done it either. I proposed it to the patient anyway, and he said, "Whatever you think is good, doctor. I trust you." It was a big responsibility, but the surgery went well.

Now the big question was whether he would regain more normal use of his hand. Within a couple of weeks his stitches were out and within six weeks he was moving the thumb. And he was strong enough that he could grab onto things. The function he obtained was incredibly helpful in many day-to-day tasks, making him much more independent. I was so grateful everything went well, and now I felt like a real plastic and reconstructive surgeon with the confidence to address other complex reconstructive challenges.

Since then I have helped reconstruct other areas of the body, especially after cancer surgery or accidents, connecting arteries, nerves and veins. I've also focused on helping patients who have lost massive amounts of weight, sometimes two hundred pounds, after gastric bypass surgery, which leaves them with extra skin that has to be cut away. This involves very complex planning and all-day surgery, but the results are dramatic and life-changing, both physically and psychologically. It is so rewarding to be able to use my skills.

I don't think most doctors appreciate what it's like to be a patient, but I have never forgotten that I was once a young girl lying helplessly on a hospital bed for three long months. I saw all the things about being a patient that aren't obvious. I learned how important it is to visit patients every day. I think I have a different outlook on what nurses do and how important they are and how hard they work. I think I'm more compassionate with people. And I think I'm better at listening to patients.

So the little girl grew up, took inspiration from the care she received, overcame early jitters as a doctor, and now is able to offer hope and understanding to her patients. It's a full circle.

My Patient, My Friend

Mark Wise

A GENERAL PRACTITIONER IS ONLY VERY rarely going to come across cases that require immediate life-saving intervention. On the other hand, those doctors who step up in a crisis may never see their patient again once the crisis has passed.

Mark Wise is a retired GP who finds it very rewarding to look back on the relationships he was able to establish with many of his patients.

My dad was a pediatrician for about fifty years. If you ask me why I became a doctor, I would say that's the default position. When your father is a doctor, maybe you'll go to medical school and become a doctor just like your dad. But there was never any pressure. I had other options, but I became a doctor.

I think if you talk to family doctors, you'll find they went into family practice for a bunch of reasons, but it wasn't that they wanted to be saving lives every second of the day. They didn't want to have people lying on the couch. They wanted to build long-term relationships. They wanted to do some preventive medicine and some curative medicine. Maybe they'd save a life along the way and maybe they'd be there for a patient during a tough time. It's like when you play baseball. You hit singles and you walk, and you make a lot of outs, but you rarely hit a grand slam home run. I think that even though family doctors are in a sort of mundane specialty, we like to hit home runs as well.

When my dad retired, he passed on some of his patients to me, and one family in particular became pretty special to me. To me that family is symbolic of the best kind of doctor–patient relationship. This was a very nice family: a mother and father who were in their mid-fifties when I met them thirty years ago, with two kids in their mid-twenties. All bright and well-educated. Sports fans. This family spent about ten or twenty years cruising along without anything much going wrong, though interestingly, Mom and Dad and daughter had the same heart murmur.

A heart murmur is a sound that can be heard with a stethoscope. The blood pumps through the heart valves like water through a pipe. Valves are meant to let blood flow in one direction and stop it from coming back, but if that valve is leaky and damaged, the blood does come back. If that's happening or if that valve is narrow, there might be an audible murmur. Just hearing it doesn't make it serious because some of these things progress and some don't. But if a patient has a critically narrowed valve and blood isn't getting through, it's going to be a problem and they'll need a new valve. If they have a tremendously leaky valve, they're pumping blood forward and it's leaking back. A person can tolerate this for quite a while, but it eventually affects the heart. The person will be tired, weak and short of breath.

Lots of people have heart murmurs, but not everyone has to worry about them. It's important to know why the murmur is there, whether it's leaky, whether it's narrow, whether it's minimal or severe. And it's very important to follow it.

At medical school, the be-all and end-all was hearing heart murmurs. We would crowd around patients with heart murmurs to listen and go to cardiologists' opulent homes to hear recordings of heart murmurs.

This family was interesting in that three of them had audible heart murmurs, so naturally I followed them closely. Once in a while, I would get students coming into my office from the local hospital, and I would bring in my interesting patients for them to see. So, this couple was constantly coming in to show off their heart murmurs. Teaching in family practice was very gratifying and very rewarding.

At one point the dad in this family had an illness with fever, chills and shakes. Ordinarily that would make me think of the flu, but because of his history with the heart murmur, I knew he would be predisposed to an infection of the valve. And that's when I hit the medical equivalent of a home run. An infected heart valve isn't always diagnosed quickly, but I did the right test right away, got him the right treatment, got him the antibiotics he needed, got him the home care that he needed and he did well.

I think the speed of the diagnosis was due to the fact that we had spent years building up a relationship. A family doctor can hope they're there and they make the right moves when they really need to, and in this case we had outstanding success. It's impossible to know what would have happened if the infection hadn't been diagnosed. It could have led to a stroke or a blood clot going to his brain or his leg or his spleen. Over time, if there was more damage to the valve, the patient could have grown sicker and sicker and potentially that infection could have become life-threatening.

After that, life went along for the family. There were the usual things: knees got creaky, there was some high cholesterol, some hair loss, some anxiety. But a few years later, the father got sick again. This time he had low back pain. One of the problems with a family practice is that really everybody comes in with the same sort of symptoms. "I have a sore back." "I have a sore knee." "I have a headache." "I'm tired." One patient has a fever. Another has a rash. Most of the time those things aren't serious.

Back pain is like that—most of the time it's a very common complaint. The patient bent over, shovelled snow, coughed, sneezed, strained a muscle. Usually a sore back is just that—a sore back. But a family doctor learns to be paranoid because they don't want to miss anything. So they look for red flags. That's why it's important to know a patient's history.

With this patient and his history of heart murmur and infected valve, I suspected a more sinister diagnosis. Sure enough, we ended up diagnosing and treating a disc infection. People get slipped discs or herniated discs, but they rarely get infected discs. I sent him back to the hospital where once again he needed prolonged antibiotics, and he got better. That was like hitting a second home run for me.

One day a few years later the mother came into my office complaining that she was out of breath. She had a history of anxiety, and a lot of people with that issue get short of breath while having a panic attack. That wasn't the problem here. I walked her up and down the stairs, and I could see how short of breath she got.

I examined her, checked her pulse. It wasn't rocket science, but I diagnosed a rapid arrhythmia, which is when your heart beats too fast. That's not efficient, and when it happens, it causes shortness of breath or light-headedness or faintness. She had all those things.

Part of a family doctor's job is to realize when somebody is sick. You see so many people who aren't sick or who are going to get better on their own, but with sick people you need to do something. First, you have to realize they're sick, and you have to do it quickly and correctly. We called an ambulance and got her to the hospital, where she was quickly treated. Her heart rate returned to normal. So that was home run number three for me with this family.

Interestingly, both Mom's and Dad's heart valves started getting worse almost simultaneously, and it became a question of who would need elective surgery first. It turned out she went in first because her case became more urgent. She had successful surgery, came home and made a full recovery. Then in order to operate on the husband, we had to wait for his wife to recover a bit because his surgery was slightly more complicated. He needed a bypass at the same time and eventually needed a pacemaker. He was a little delirious after the surgery, so it was quite rocky in the coronary care unit. I remember going to visit the family there, which brings in another role of the family doctor—just being with the family during a very stressful time.

Part of the reason a doctor goes into family practice is because he's not like the surgeon. Surgeons aren't there to talk to people. They're there to give them a new knee or take out an appendix. Family doctors learn about their patients as people. They can talk about hockey or grandchildren or work or stamp collecting or music. A family doctor who's lucky has a constant flow of friends coming into the office, and it's nice to have these relationships.

I recently went to the funeral of a ninety-seven-year-old patient who died with dementia. We had known each other for forty years, from good times to bad times. He had a solid handshake, and always a nice smile. At his funeral I sat beside his Filipino caregiver and I listened to eulogies by his two sons, and I thought, this is what family practice is all about: looking after people through thick and thin and being there right until the end.

That's the way it has been with the family I've been talking about. I went out for lunch with the father last week, and we reminisced about days gone by. With some patients you break the barrier and go beyond the impersonal contact. For me the joy of family practice wasn't putting people on Lipitor to lower their cholesterol. It was establishing a bond. The joy was in meeting with a friend at Tim Hortons—a friend who just happened to be my patient.

Brain Reset

Paul Atkinson

DOCTORS GO TO WORK EVERY DAY hoping they can employ the skills and techniques that produce the best results for their patients. They count on their research and experience to guide them, yet they are aware that some things in medicine are still mysterious and can't be explained.

Paul Atkinson is an emergency doctor at Saint John Regional Hospital in New Brunswick. He grew up in Northern Ireland and first practised emergency medicine in Cambridge, England, where he once had an unforgettable day.

One of the issues emergency physicians have to get used to is not knowing what happens to patients. They come in with a minor problem or something moderately bad or something catastrophic. I deal with their problems and most times I don't see them again. I just don't hear much about what happens once they leave the emergency department.

I often have an idea that I've helped someone, and occasionally I get a card or a note that says, "Thank you," but most times I just move on. But one case stands out in my mind as being one of those moments when I thought: Well, there you go! I think I helped make someone's life better just because I happened to be lucky enough to be in the right spot at that time, and I did my job.

It was the case of young lady we'll call Nicola. I knew nothing about her when she came to Emergency, of course, but I found out later she was nineteen years old and a student at a local community college. She wasn't really into school, though—not at all engaged. You might say she was trying to be a student. She'd had a depression diagnosis for some time and had threatened to end her life. She had been in and out of care with psychiatrists and mental health teams, and had struggled with substance abuse at times. She had real troubles.

I was in the emergency room in the late afternoon when paramedics brought Nicola in as a poisoning self-harm—an attempted suicide. At that point it was an almost successful suicide. When she arrived, she was in cardiac arrest, and the paramedics were doing CPR on her. As you might imagine, this is not a hopeful situation—the outcome is usually poor. I led the resuscitation team, which consisted of a couple of nurses, another doctor and the paramedics, and we worked on Nicola very aggressively, trying to get her heart to beat.

I diagnosed an overdose based on the circumstantial evidence I had. We knew she had been on tricyclic antidepressants, which are extremely dangerous as they can affect the heart and central nervous system, and they can reduce blood pressure. They are not commonly used anymore because we now have safer drugs with fewer side effects. In Nicola's case they had essentially put her into an arrhythmia—an abnormal heart rhythm—which we couldn't get her out of no matter what we did. We used electrical shocks. We gave her large volumes of sodium bicarbonate, which is the antidote. But nothing was working.

For fifty-five minutes we tried to resuscitate her, and we had arrived at the point where we really were starting to lose hope. A drug overdose is one of the circumstances where the advice is to go longer than normal, but the average length of time we would try to resuscitate would probably be twenty minutes or maybe a half-hour. Doubling or tripling that length of time can cause serious worries about the state of the patient's brain. I was starting to be really concerned. Even if she could survive, what sort of state would she survive in? After almost an hour of resuscitation, I was concerned that she might end up in a persistent vegetative state or at least have severe cognitive impairment. But we kept trying because Nicola was young, and a young person has an increased chance of survival. Not a much bigger chance, mind you. It goes from minuscule to small, but that's still something. So we kept going. However, I knew that one way or another, we were close to the end.

Her family was brought to the hospital, and as my team continued trying to resuscitate, I excused myself from the family and stepped back inside the trauma room. I could see a change in the rhythm on the ECG monitor. I felt her pulse. We were starting to get her back. We carried on, and within ten or fifteen minutes more we had a strong pulse. We had a blood pressure. We were able to get her stabilized and transfer her to the intensive care unit for ongoing management. It was a great save and normally that would have been the end of things. As an emergency doctor, I wouldn't hear anything more about her.

But the most remarkable part of the story was still to come. Nicola was in intensive care for three or four days, and as she was stabilized and weaned off the ventilator, she became fully conscious. As I said, we were worried that she might have suffered irreparable brain damage while we were trying to resuscitate her. Even if it wasn't catastrophic, I thought there might be some cognitive impairment, some disability. But she awoke fully alert. She was perfectly clear. Even more amazingly, she was no longer depressed. She had suffered for years with depression. Now she woke up from the nightmare. The circumstances of her life were still the same, but she truly had an elevated mood. She had no memory of the past months. It was as if her brain had been reset.

I had heard of this happening but had never seen it. Something that occurred during the resuscitation had changed everything for her. Whether it was the medications we had used during the cardiac arrest or the electric shocks, she had experienced a complete reset during the prolonged period of disruption in neuro function in the brain.

She went home, and I remember receiving a communication from her family some months later saying she was doing extremely well, was re-engaged in her education and had not slipped back into depression.

I've treated thousands of people over the years, and I can tell stories about all kinds of weird and wonderful conditions I've seen. Strange diagnoses, cool tests and times I've been proud of picking up on something another doctor might have missed. But this case stands out. For me it was pivotal. I realized that even if I didn't see what happened to most patients beyond the emergency room, I could always have hope that things would work out okay, that perhaps I could actually move people from a really dark place in their lives to something better.

Nicola's case happened relatively early in my career as an emergency physician, and it reinforced a couple of things. The first was that I was dealing with people and their lives. It wasn't just a body in front of me. Emergency care has consequences. The second was that it made me focus on the need to truly be the best I could be. When you are trying to resuscitate someone, it's not a situation where you can afford to fail. There are only two possible outcomes: life and death. I think sometimes maybe we give up a little too early in resuscitation for fear that we will cause harm. This was an example to me that it's not always the case. Persisting, carrying on beyond what the guidelines say, going the extra mile, can be a good thing at times.

This case jumps out over all the other cases I've seen over the past fifteen years. I can see the exact setting. I can see the family, remember the drugs we gave Nicola, and I can still see the heart monitor. It really stands out.

Dying on a Bed of Roses

Photo by Dodge Baena

George Ibrahim

REQUIESCAT IN PACE. REST IN PEACE. IT'S our wish for those who have died. Some people facing death, however, aren't thinking that far ahead. Their greatest wish is to *die* in peace.

George Ibrahim is a pediatric neurosurgeon at the Hospital for Sick Children in Toronto. He found out early in his career that while medical practice is about science, it's also about much more than that.

My background is in science. I was in biochemistry, interested in research and looking to do a PhD. I was not at all interested in medicine, but during my undergraduate training I realized that research and medicine are kind of inseparable. You can have much more insight into the human body and diseases and potentially have much more impact if you understand both of those worlds. So I went into medicine.

When I finished med school, I started my neurosurgery residency, but in that same year I also rotated through other specialties. At one point I was rotating through internal medicine, and I discovered there are significant cultural differences between this specialty and surgery. In surgery we pride ourselves on being efficient, diligent, matter-of-fact, pragmatic. That's our approach to patient care. We see a problem, address the problem, the problem goes away, and we move on to the next problem. It's part of our organizational thinking when we approach a surgery. Everything is systematic, compartmentalized and organized in a very specific way.

Internal medicine has some similarities, of course, but the patient population is more complex. One patient can have multiple conditions, so everything is more cumbersome. Older patients, especially, may have many more illnesses, each of which needs to be addressed individually and in combination with everything else.

One classic example is medications. A medication given to treat one condition can have side effects on other conditions. For example, if someone has heart disease you might prescribe a diuretic to rid the body of excess water, which makes it easier for the heart to pump. But if that same person has kidney disease, it could make that worse. It's very time-consuming because the doctor needs to provide a lot more care when it comes to understanding the illness he's treating and how it relates to all the patient's other illnesses.

During my internal medicine rotation, I treated one lady who remains the most complex patient I've come across in my entire medical career. She was in her sixties, so she wasn't old per se, but she had truly significant medical issues. According to her list of medical problems, which was at least a page and a half long, she had problems in almost every organ in her body. She had an auto-immune condition that had affected multiple organs. Her kidney issues were so severe she was on dialysis. She also had cardiac issues. And each of those conditions interacted with another, so it was exceedingly complex. I spent three or four hours going through her charts, trying to understand the history of each of her medical conditions. It was a real effort on my part to disentangle the differ-ent issues so that I had a clear understanding of everything in my mind before I felt ready to talk to her.

When I went into her room to see her, I was feeling very proud of myself for having spent the time to figure out her illnesses. She wasn't impressed. She had no interest whatsoever in talking about any of her medical conditions. No interest at all. I had spent hours reading her charts, only to discover that she was not even a little engaged in her own health care. Because although I had spent three hours reading through her charts, she had spent the last three years of her life living those charts. It had taken quite a toll on her. All she wanted to do was pass away peacefully.

As I was the primary person assigned to her care, over the fol-lowing weeks I spent a fair bit of time with her. She was immobile and bedbound. For the last several years of her life she had been essentially confined to a hospital. I think she recognized that no amount of medical intervention would afford her the quality of life that, in her mind, would make her life worth living. She had decided to refuse any further medical treatment, which included dialysis. This would lead to certain death.

She was completely lucid when she made the decision, and I thought it was a decision that a reasonable person in her frame of mind, having lived through her experiences, could make. Refusing life-supporting treatment was certainly within her prerogative, and it wasn't up to me or anyone else to try to change her mind. We explored the factors she was weighing and her state of mind when she made her decision. Was she depressed? Was some other potentially remediable factor affecting her decision? Were we unaware if an additional condition that could be playing into this? But the truth was that she wasn't depressed and nothing else was going on either. She just felt that the quality of her life was not what she wanted.

We talked quite a bit and she told me how much she liked music. Her favourite song was Jon Bon Jovi's "Bed of Roses." I thought much later that maybe some of the lyrics fit her situation. He sings about someone sleeping on a bed of nails, and wanting to lay them down in a bed of roses.

I think the single most valuable thing I did to contribute to her health care was to make her a CD with that song on it as well as other Bon Jovi songs she liked.

Without the dialysis, she died of renal failure. Afterward I met with her two adult children, and the gratitude they expressed was really special for me. I think they appreciated that we had made sure their mother was comfortable and not in pain and well taken care of. But I think they were most grateful that I had taken the time to understand her and what she valued. It's one thing to give medications to keep someone comfortable. It's another thing to make a CD of her favourite songs so that she was not just physically but also emotionally and mentally comfortable, that she felt understood and valued and appreciated. I think that is where their gratitude came from.

I've had many adrenalin-filled, trauma-based patient encounters, cases where we worked really hard to resuscitate someone who—by all the measures we use to quantify risk of death—should not have lived. I saw a teenage girl who came in after a car accident one night with multiple organs failing. She had lost her heart rhythm and needed active resuscitation multiple times. She had brain injury, spine injury, rib injury, abdominal injury and broken bones. We didn't think she would make it to the next morning. But she came through, and a year later was walking around without a scratch. Unforgettable? Of course.

But the story of the woman who just wanted a peaceful end to her life reminds me of why I became a doctor in a more poignant and personal way.

As a postscript, her kids told me their mother died while listening to "Bed of Roses" on the CD I made for her.

New and Improved

Shady Ashamalla

IN THE ADVERTISING INDUSTRY THE words "new and improved" are tossed around every time a new scent is added to a laundry detergent or a toothpaste is packaged in a new tube. In medicine there's not a whole lot of advertising.

Shady Ashamalla is a surgical oncologist at Sunnybrook Hospital's Odette Cancer Centre. When he started performing a "new and improved" procedure, he didn't exactly advertise it, but he did try to get the word out.

When I was finishing my training, the chief here at the hospital said, "If you do a fellowship in both minimally invasive surgery and surgical oncology, you'll be the first to marry those two fields, and it's what we need here." He liked to use vivid catch phrases to express his sentiments, and he said, "We're inventing the future of health care. If you combine these two things, I'll make a job for you."

So off I went. I did a fellowship in both those things, and true to his word he hired me. I came to the hospital with a very clear mandate to do minimally invasive colorectal cancer surgery. That was several years ago, and to this day there really aren't many doctors in the country who have a practice as limited as mine. I say that because a lot of other cancer surgeons do a lot of other types of cancer, and a lot of the minimally invasive surgeons do a lot of other kinds of minimally invasive surgery. There are very few who just do both as their entire practice.

When I started, it was hard to know how it was going to go. Was I going to run out of gas? Was I going to be bored? It's a very limited, specialized practice, but the technology was evolving, so I put a lot of effort into taking it to the next level. The concept was to use laparoscopic surgery, using minimally invasive surgery, to remove rectal cancers through the anus. The term "laparoscopic" applies to placing a laparoscope or camera into a body cavity and then using long, thin instruments to operate while looking at what you're doing through the camera's image, not directly with your eyes. Doctors had used this technology for many years to take out gallbladders or appendixes. Now we were going to use it to take out cancers.

The people who invented this technique were in Orlando, Florida, so I went to Orlando and spent time there learning all I could. But when I brought it back to Toronto, I faced tons of resistance. Other hospitals and other centres at the University of Toronto said, "You shouldn't be doing this. This hasn't been cleared." I went to my surgeon-in-chief and the CEO of the hospital and asked, "Should I continue with this? Is this something we should proceed with?"

They were really adamant that I should continue. They told me, "The science is there. You're an early adopter, so people are going to resist it, but if you feel it's better for patients, and if you think you're making a positive impact, then go for it. We'll support you."

So we went ahead, but it was hard because we knew we were being watched very closely.

One patient stands out in my mind who completely justified the entire process, justified all the struggles we went through to bring this technology to Canada. He was a young man, just forty-three years old, and he had shown up one day at the emergency department of a different hospital with rectal bleeding. The emergency physician there did a rectal exam, felt a mass and referred him to the surgeon on call. The surgeon saw him, did a few tests, including a biopsy, CT scan and MRI, and then sent the patient home until the results could be interpreted.

When the man came back to see the surgeon, the news wasn't good. The surgeon was very straightforward. He told the patient, "You have rectal cancer. The only way to get this cancer out is to remove your rectum and your anus. We do that through a large open incision in your abdomen. We make a big up-and-down cut about a foot and a half long in your abdomen. There'll be an incision where your anus used to be that will be closed off, and you'll have a permanent pouch for stool for the rest of your life."

This was a forty-three-year-old man. He was obviously devastated. He could have just accepted what he was told, but instead he went online to try to find an alternative. He found us. He found the clinic I had created, the Young Adult Colorectal Cancer Clinic. We were targeting patients under the age of fifty who had just been diagnosed with colorectal cancer. We had put a lot of effort into reaching out to patients, into reaching out to family physicians, so that we were findable online.

This man sent us an email, and our nurse navigators instructed him how to come in for a consultation. We reviewed everything from scratch. We examined him with a scope. We biopsied the mass. We did an ultrasound, an MRI and a CT scan. When we were completely done, we reviewed the results with our team, and only then did we tell the patient that we had an alternative way to remove his cancer.

Because it was an early stage rectal cancer, we thought it would be safe to excise it locally. Just cut it out through the bum, a process that doesn't mean removal of the rectum or the anus. It doesn't mean any incision in the abdomen at all. No pouch for stool. Less pain and less pain medication. The patient goes home the same day and life goes on. We were certain that from a cancer perspective, there would be no compromise to his outcome. Obviously, the man was thrilled with this alternative.

It was day surgery. He came in. We brought him to the operating room and cut out the cancer in about an hour and a half. It all went very, very well. He went home that same day and three or four days later he was out walking. No issues at all. No incisions to heal, nothing. And he was cured. I have been seeing him every year since then. We're now five years out and the risk window for a recurrence of his rectal cancer is gone.

I would never say his treatment would have been worse at the first hospital he went to. If he'd had the operation there, he would have been cured of his cancer. The biggest threat to his life was the cancer, but when you think about what was going to be done to his body, that's where I feel pretty good. Because he looked for an alternative and found us, this man's life took a completely different pathway. We had profoundly reduced the level of trauma that had to occur in order to cure him, and that made me really proud of what we had created. It made me very happy that I had pursued the entire course of training and then implemented these things in my practice instead of just going with the status quo. I had a patient whose life was dramatically better because we did things differently.

The noninvasive approach is much more widespread now. We developed a two-year course to bring it to other places, and all that resistance to early adoption quickly became an eagerness to learn, which is great. But this technique is limited to early stage rectal cancer, which means you have to find the cancer before it's too late. The standard guideline for having a colonoscopy says to begin at age fifty, but I literally see two or three new colorectal cancer patients in my clinic every week who are younger than fifty. So people should learn the symptoms and get checked out if something seems wrong.

The Number One Health Threat

Courtney Howard

Photo by Pat Kane

YOU DON'T BECOME A DOCTOR overnight. It's a minimum ten years of post-secondary education, and for some specialties and subspecialties you can tack on another nine years or so before you're ready to practise. It's exhaustive and exhausting. And yet maybe something is missing.

Courtney Howard is an emergency doctor in Yellowknife. She is also the president of Canadian Association of Physicians for the Environment. She was surprised to find out what she hadn't learned in medical school.

I trained in British Columbia and Quebec. I originally came north because I wanted to work for Doctors Without Borders. They said, "Okay, if you want to work with us, you should go work in the Canadian North first because you'll get used to working with culturally diverse populations in a more remote setting, and you'll get used to working without a CT scanner."

So, there I was on my way to Inuvik. I had just finished about fifteen years in an academic medical environment and a hospital. I had been so focused on gaining medical knowledge, and it had consumed so much of my time, that I felt I had basically no "outside" knowledge. Now I was trying to read more broadly so I could feel more like an adult.

At the airport in Edmonton, waiting to change planes, I picked up a book about climate change. It wasn't quite a whim, but I wasn't a committed environmentalist either. I bought the book just because it seemed like something important to learn about. I read it mostly in Inuvik in the depths of winter. It's dark there at that time of year, of course, and it's the kind of place where you can get into a serious topic. There aren't a lot of distractions.

I became quite alarmed about climate change, and in medicine what we are taught to do when we learn something new is to review the existing literature. So I went to the medical literature. This was just a few months after the *Lancet*, the world's oldest and most prestigious medical journal, had issued a report saying that climate change was "the biggest global health threat of the 21st century." I had just finished training at McGill, one of Canada's top universities with a fantastic medical program, yet they had never mentioned this. I thought: What? How did we miss the number one health threat? So I got involved in climate change and health at the start of the field—or close to the beginning—and I have worked in that area quite a lot since then. I've done research and advocacy work, all while living in Canada's North, where we've now learned the climate is warming at three times the global rate.

This is not an abstraction for me. The majority of my patients are Indigenous. Many of them still get a substantial amount of their calories from hunting on the land. Climate change can mean less access to wildlife and more safety risks from changes in the thickness of the sea ice. Traditional food security may be significantly affected. And it doesn't stop there. Climate change can bring animals into greater contact with people, causing more disease. Extreme weather is dangerous. Even visiting friends and family in remote communities is affected when ice roads aren't stable.

The College of Family Physicians has four principles for family practice. One of them is to be a resource to your client population, which means doing more than just seeing people when they come in the door. Of course, clinical medicine is my bread and butter so I love going to the emergency department to serve people. But I'm living in one of the most rapidly warming places in the world and my patients are telling me, "Look, this is really impacting my life"; then as somebody who was trained in the Canadian medical system, it is my duty to bring the physician's voice to bear on the situation. I must be an advocate for my patients at the community level, at the national level and even at the international level.

I have been connecting with other doctors in Canada and internationally, while at the same time I've had a very interesting collaboration with some of our Indigenous leaders. Francois Paulette was chief of the Elders Council at our hospital, and he's incredibly well known internationally. He's done research on integrating traditional Indigenous knowledge with Western science, and he's usually the Elder who represents Canada at international climate change negotiations. I've had the privilege of being with him at these negotiations, where he introduces me as *his* doctor or as a doctor from his territory. Another neighbour who has been at the climate change negotiations is Bill Erasmus, who is now the Honorary National Chief of the Dene Nation for Life. He lives just down the road from me, but I originally met him at my very first protest. Francois speaks very powerfully on the impact climate change is having on his traditional life and about Indigenous healers and their declining ability to gather traditional medicines from the land.

At the 2015 United Nations Climate Change Conference in Paris (or COP21, which stands for Conference of Parties, meaning the countries that signed the UN Framework on Climate Change), Francois opened up the Indigenous Peoples Pavilion. I was allowed to sit with them at the smudging ceremony to cleanse the room and the participants, and then I listened as Indigenous People from around the world talked about the impact of climate change on them. I knew most of the doctors at that conference, but none of them were in that room, and I felt that room should have been packed with doctors listening.

Two years later I was at COP23 in Germany and spent a lot of time there with Bill and Francois. They invited me to watch their deliberations with Indigenous leaders from other countries. Think about that. Canada goes to negotiate for Canada, but the Indigenous delegation represents people from all over the world. It is the most diverse-looking group of people you have ever seen in your life, and they have to come to consensus before they can go to negotiate as one in front of the rest of the international community. As a physician from Canada's North, just watching that was really inspiring for me because the Indigenous population from my community was showing leadership on the global stage.

A little later I was part of Canada's biggest event of the conference. Canada and the United Kingdom had decided to co-found the Powering Past Coal Alliance, which is a commitment to eliminate coal power by 2030, and they were trying to get other governments to sign on. This was a very big deal as coal power is one of the major targets of the health community, and I was chosen to represent the voice of health at the announcement. It was the moment when I thought, this is exactly what I should be doing. I had that really distinct thought, and I felt it stronger then than at any other point in my medical career.

I had been given a platform to communicate to the world with my neighbours, my teachers and members of my patient population sitting beside me. It was one of the greatest honours I have had in my life. Dealing with climate change within a health framework is the most effective way of motivating people into action, and physicians and nurses tend to top the list of trusted messengers. So there I was at the biggest forum in the world as a trusted messenger for my nation's biggest announcement, advocating on what I believe is the biggest problem in the world. It felt like I was hitting the absolute sweet spot in terms of the impact that a physician can have on health, not only for the current generation but for future generations. That was a moment when I sat there feeling, this is why I'm a doctor.

If we don't get our greenhouse gas emissions under control, we are going to a place that threatens not only health care but health care structures. Look at the emergency evacuation of the Fort McMurray hospital in 2016 because of the wildfires and what that meant for patients there. That kind of thing is only going to increase. Look at Hurricane Maria in Puerto Rico, which took out one of the world's largest manufacturers of sterile bags of saline solution, leading to IV bag shortages in faraway Yellowknife. Look at Syria, which had a functioning health care system until five years of climate-related drought brought famine and rural-to-urban population displacement. This in turn became one of the primary factors precipitating their long civil war, during which they've gone from having a working health care system to having bombed-out hospitals.

Doctors are used to facing urgent situations, and they're trained to handle those situations by focusing on getting things done and getting them done now. As more doctors come to realize that climate change is a health emergency, they must come to represent more and more of the leadership in getting climate change under control.

Solving the Puzzle

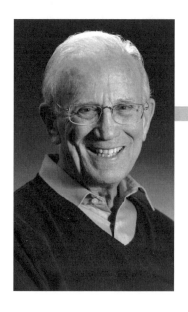

Arthur Bookman

WHEN A DOCTOR STARTS LISTENING TO A patient with a complaint, it's sometimes the equivalent of opening a box with a jigsaw puzzle inside. There are a lot of pieces, but until you start to put them together, they don't mean very much. And it isn't until you get all the pieces to fit that you have a complete picture.

Arthur Bookman is a rheumatologist, someone who specializes in diseases that affect the joints, tendons, ligaments, bones and muscles. He remembers a patient with symptoms that were particularly difficult to diagnose.

My patient, a clerical worker in his forties, had a history of asthma. Now he was getting aches and pains, and nobody quite knew what was wrong with him.

One day he landed in the hospital because he had developed diarrhea, and after a while they realized his pancreas wasn't working. They gave him supplements to help him digest his food and that made him feel better, but still no one understood what was going on. Why was he having these symptoms? When his aches and pains got worse, he was referred to me.

People become very frustrated when something is wrong with them and doctors are saying, "Well, I can't find anything." Then maybe the doctor asks, "Are you anxious? Is something going on in your family?" And sometimes that is the answer. Probably more times than not there are things going on in your life that can cause physical symptoms, and if you gain control of your life, the symptoms will go away.

But sometimes there's a disease, and a doctor has to be able to tell the difference. The history of asthma and increasing aches and pains along with the new symptoms suggested I should check for inflammation. I did a few blood tests, and realized that, indeed, there was a lot of inflammation going on in his body. Then I remembered reading that one of the reasons your pancreas can suddenly fail is if the blood vessels in your body are inflamed. It's a relatively rare condition called "polyarteritis," and if that was his problem, the blood supply to the pancreas had been cut off, so it had died.

I admitted him to the hospital and did some more blood tests. Based on those results we biopsied one his muscles—that is, we took a piece of the muscle and looked at the tissue, blood vessels, veins and connective tissue. We discovered that his muscle wasn't inflamed, but the artery was inflamed. So he did indeed have polyarteritis.

A blood vessel that gets irritated and inflamed can clot, and pieces of the body can suddenly lose their blood supply, so the patient comes to the doctor with a series of mysterious events. For example, he can have a stroke or get a gangrenous finger or a sudden blood clot in the kidney. In the case of the kidney, he feels pain and the kidney has sort of shut down. If the bowel suddenly loses its blood supply, it can produce a real catastrophe.

So any part of the body where there's an artery—which is every part of the body—can suddenly lose its blood supply. And it usually happens in little bits and pieces in a process that evolves over time. It doesn't happen in a day or two, like something that suddenly appears and causes violent illness. You can be walking around but losing weight and not understanding why. It can sneak up on you, as it did with this patient.

With my diagnosis confirmed, I started my patient on cortisone and he seemed to do very well. I thought: Great! We're out of the woods. We didn't realize at the time that cortisone wasn't the whole answer for managing this condition.

About a year and a half or maybe two years later, this patient came to Emergency with severe stomach pain. The emergency doctors called the surgeon, who put a needle into the patient's belly and struck blood. The patient was hemorrhaging from something. When they couldn't figure out from what, the surgeon called to ask what I thought. I had no idea, so he took the patient to the operating room and discovered he was bleeding from around his gallbladder.

The surgeon removed the gallbladder, but then saw there was blood oozing out around the liver and patched it up to try to stop the bleeding. Then they sent the man to the recovery room, at which point his blood pressure dropped! So, they took him to the x-ray department and discovered the blood vessels throughout his abdomen had aneurysms—that is, they had bulges in them.

All this was from the polyarteritis, which had been quietly progressing. When he first came to us with the pancreas problem and the muscle pain, his body had already been forming all these aneurysms—these bulges. One of them had now burst in his liver and was hemorrhaging into his gut right through his liver. So they put in a little device to block the artery to his liver. Of course, half his liver died because it didn't have a blood supply, but the remainder of his liver was viable. So, they let him out of the hospital.

At this point I saw research describing the use of a cancer drug that could be effective for polyarteritis. I put him on the drug and followed him for a while, and he did wonderfully. But then he stopped coming into my office.

We all get busy and don't necessarily call people to come back. And he had a family doctor, who I knew would send him back to me if necessary. About five years later his family doctor did send him back to me because he had blood in his urine. I was devastated to find that he was still on the cancer drug because in the meantime, we had started to learn that we couldn't keep patients on that drug forever. They had to get off after six months to a year because it could actually cause cancer.

That's the nature of these drugs. They stop the cancer from growing, but sometimes they can make the cells start growing abnormally. So it looked as if the drug that had helped him for one disease had caused him to get bladder cancer. We took him into the hospital again and tried to get the cancer out but it was too late. He ultimately died.

I've never known why he stopped coming to me. I think he may just have wanted to put it all behind him. Maybe he just decided, "Okay, I'm done now. I don't have to think about all this anymore." What I do know is that he was a mystery and we figured out the mystery. We prolonged his life. We gave him at least another five or six years after the diagnosis was made.

As a rheumatologist part of what I do is treat patients, and that gives me great satisfaction, but it's hard to give the person proper treatment unless the diagnosis is correct. For common diseases that is usually easy because we see these things all the time. But when something is a little rarer and it doesn't present in an obvious manner, many doctors miss what's going on.

In this case the man had polyarteritis, a relatively rare disorder. It wasn't until a lot of different things happened that we started to think outside the box and ask: Why is this person having pancreas issues along with aching muscles? Is there a connection to his background with asthma? What is happening inside this one person? What explanation pulls all these facts together?

Being the doctor who can draw on special training, who can look at something in a way nobody else has and figure it out—that gives me a great amount of satisfaction.

The High Cost
of Stigma

Vincent Agyapong

THE CALENDAR TELLS US THAT WE ARE IN the early part of the twenty-first century, but all over the world people retain attitudes ingrained in their societies many hundreds of years ago. Very often those ancient attitudes cause tangible and terrible harm.

Vincent Agyapong is a psychiatrist who works at the Community Mental Health section of Alberta Health Services in Edmonton. He is fighting an uphill battle for better mental health care in his native land, the West African country of Ghana.

I trained for psychiatry in Ireland, and after I finished my training in 2008, I went back home to Ghana and thought seriously about staying. But I had to take my family into account. I have a wife and three children, and it wouldn't be easy making a living as a psychiatrist in Ghana. Psychiatry is highly stigmatized there. You can get an idea of how unimportant it was considered at that time—how unnecessary—when I tell you that in the entire country, which had a population then of about twenty-five million people, there were only four psychiatrists. And if you looked at those four psychiatrists, you would see four old men with grey hair and broken-down cars. They were very poor. There was nothing flamboyant about them. If you went to one of the mental institutions in which they worked, you would see terrible conditions.

I was really conflicted. I knew it would look like I was being selfish if I decided to return to Europe. And I really wanted to contribute to my country. On the other hand, I had to think of my family. I finally came up with a solution to my personal dilemma. I thought I could go back to Europe but work to increase the number of psychiatrists in Ghana.

First I committed to going to Ghana every year to teach at a medical school. I could try to give hope to young medical students and young doctors and inspire them to specialize in psychiatry. Around the same time the Ghana College of Physicians and Surgeons was established, and they opened a faculty of psychiatry with the four local psychiatrists and some international faculty. I thought I could help with the training, and I came up with the idea of a contest among the four medical schools in the country to send a group of students for training abroad. I thought it was very important to give a new image to psychiatry. If I could send young medical students away from Ghana to see how psychiatry is practised elsewhere, it would help instill in them a sense of self-worth. It would make them believe they could change psychiatry in Ghana.

I obtained some funding from St. Patrick's Mental Health Services in Dublin, Ireland's largest, independent, not-for-profit mental health service, which is almost three hundred years old. We got support from the new Ghana College of Physicians and Surgeons and from all the departments of psychiatry at the medical schools in Ghana. In 2010 we launched what we called the Inter-Medical School Public Speaking Competition and got scholarships for two winners and two runners-up. That first year the competitors would speak about the funding of medical health in Ghana. There was a big media campaign around the launch so that Ghana's general public became aware of the competition, and we got the national TV network to cover the event. It was broadcast live across the entire nation from the capital city, Accra.

With two speakers from each of the medical schools, and with a national television audience, it became a big platform to get improvement for mental health in the country. We sponsored the four winners to travel to Dublin to participate in a four-week elective program at St. Patrick's University Hospital and St. John of God Hospital, the two leading mental health hospitals in Dublin.

We managed to sustain our funding, so we have held the competition every year since then. Last year we decided to evaluate how we were doing. We wanted to see if we had achieved what we set out to achieve—more medical students training in psychiatry. And guess what? The number of psychiatrists in Ghana has increased from four in 2010 when we started the competition to twenty-four today. In addition, we have about twenty-six doctors doing residency training in psychiatry.

It's by no means enough. In Edmonton, where I now work, about two hundred and fifty psychiatrists serve a population of about a million people, whereas in Ghana twenty-four psychiatrists serve a population of about thirty million. It's nowhere close to what is needed but it's still a giant step to have moved from four to twenty-four in about a decade.

Was the competition responsible for the increase? We handed out surveys to medical students, physicians, other medical professionals and journalists to find out. Almost 80 per cent of the medical students agreed that the competition had helped to positively change their perception of psychiatry. About 60 per cent agreed that they would be more interested in becoming psychiatrists because of the competition. We published the results in the *Journal of Academic Psychiatry*.

We didn't stop with the competition. It occurred to me that it would be a good idea not just to train people to become psychiatrists but to train an army of global mental health practitioners—people well versed with the knowledge and skills to develop and evaluate mental health programs. I sought the support of the World Health Organization as well as international partners like the University of Alberta, the University of Alabama and St. Patrick's University in Dublin. I designed a curriculum for a master's program in global mental health policy services and development, submitted it to the University of Ghana and obtained accreditation from the academic board of the university.

We launched the program last year. We currently have seventeen students—sixteen from Ghana and one from Nigeria. We have two intensive residential sessions. I teach in the second session along with faculty from Canada, the US, the UK and Ireland. Between the two sessions, the students participate in online distance learning under the direction of faculty from around the world. We are hoping to get people from other countries to enrol in this program as well.

Unfortunately, the government in Ghana has not helped at all. It is not interested in anything that will not fetch votes, and mental health has been a victim of this attitude. If the government had wanted to improve things, it would have to come up with a commitment to fund mental health programs. We have tried to pressure the government to at least decriminalize attempted suicide, but it remains a criminal offence, so someone who tries to end their life goes to jail instead of to hospital. Nothing we have said on this subject has translated into any tangible impact on the government.

Truth be told, there isn't a huge groundswell of protest in Ghana about the lack of mental health facilities. The stigma against being seen as advocating for psychiatric care is too great. A few years back I raised some money to donate to one of the psychiatric hospitals, and I asked one of my classmates to accompany me to make the donation. She said, "No, I don't want to be seen on TV donating to a psychiatric hospital because people are going to think I have a psychiatric problem myself." That's how strong the stigma is.

So we have made progress, but there is a long way to go yet. I have remained in Canada, but I continue to contribute to the development of mental health programs in Ghana. I go back twice a year to impart knowledge—to train people to see more patients—which I believe is more impactful than going back to see patients. So that is my greatest joy, and honestly that is my greatest satisfaction in being a doctor.

Changing a Life in an Instant

Stan Feinberg

DOCTORS OFTEN SEE PATIENTS IN TIMES of their deepest distress. They can be in both physical and mental difficulty when faced with life-altering medical procedures, and when caring for them, doctors have to be mindful of both their physical and emotional state.

Stan Feinberg is a colorectal surgeon and chief of staff at North York General Hospital. He has seen patients in despair make remarkable recoveries.

I got into medical school when I was quite young, and I really didn't know what I was getting into. Along the way I had a rotation on surgery. I was working with a couple of very charismatic, very special individuals, and I really enjoyed working with them. Pretty soon I started operating, and it was interesting to me to see a guy come in with a bowel obstruction or bleeding from his gut or even with cancer and realize I could make a big impact in a relatively short period of time. Within three or four days this individual's life could be turned around. That made an impression on me.

I still experience this suddenness in the effect my work can have on people. Last night I was on call, and it was a quiet evening so I went home and went to bed at about 11:30. I was very tired. Just after midnight I got a call from my resident, who told me there was a patient in Emergency. As soon as she gave me a few details, I knew I would have to operate on this guy, and probably soon. I went back to the hospital, saw this older man, and knew if I didn't operate on him immediately he'd be dead within a day. So I was up most of the night with this patient, and today he's fine.

I've been practising now for about thirty-two years, and I don't think I've ever been bored, not even for one day, which is kind of nice. When I do administrative work, I sometimes go to a meeting and struggle to stay awake. But with the clinical stuff, there's never a problem.

Sometimes I operate on somebody with cancer, let's say, and while I'm operating, I figure this person is not going to do well. Things are so bad they may even die. But then five years later I see them in my office and think, this man or this woman is still doing great. That's an amazing feeling. I remember once I had a patient with a terrible cancer. I would have predicted she would have died, but maybe a dozen years later I was picking up my son, who was playing with a friend. I walked into the house and the woman inside said, "You don't recognize me." It was that same woman, quite alive.

I remember operating on a super-nice man in his mid-twenties. At about five foot nine inches tall and only eighty pounds, he looked dreadful. I had to take out his whole colon, which meant that when I was done, he didn't have control of his waste—he would need a pouch for the rest of his life. I figured that would be a disaster for this young guy, but about a year later he sent me a picture of himself finishing the Toronto Marathon. He was wearing shorts and he had huge muscles. He was really built. It was a complete turnaround. He was enjoying every aspect of his life, and he said to me, "If you ever have a patient who's going through what I went through and needs to speak to someone, I'm happy to do it." And since this patient comes from a visible minority, he also said, "And if you ever have a patient from a different cultural group, it might be helpful for them to speak to someone like me." It's heartening to see people who really adjust, even if it's a long road back to health.

Another patient who had to come a long way back to health was a young woman, about eighteen years old, who had been sick for about four years with ulcerative colitis. Now she had cancer, too. Ulcerative colitis is an autoimmune illness. We don't quite understand why people get it, but it causes severe inflammation in the colon—so much that it impairs the body's ability to absorb nutrients from food. If it's very bad, they can lose twenty or thirty pounds in a month, literally wasting away. Patients with ulcerative colitis can also have a lot of bleeding and lose a lot of blood.

The drugs this young woman had been taking for her colitis worked by suppressing her immune system, so her cancer was more aggressive than it might otherwise have been. But neither she nor her family could get their heads around the type of surgery required to make her better because it would mean a stoma—that is, like the young man I referred to earlier, her waste would be collected in a pouch outside her body. The thought of that was too much for them to bear.

When I saw her, she was physically and emotionally drained and debilitated. She was incredibly thin, weighing only about seventy-five pounds. Without major surgery she was going to die, but still she and her family couldn't deal with it. They thought this would be the end of the world. But they came to realize there really was no choice. They agreed to the operation, and as far as the surgery went, it was a success. The question now was how she would recover emotionally, but I'm pleased to say she bounced back remarkably well. It's five years later and when she comes in now, I see a young woman who looks perfectly healthy. You would never guess she has the pouch. She has a career and friends, and her life is back on track. She's enjoying herself. She had undergone surgery that she really didn't want, but it saved her life.

One Christmas Eve when I was trying to get out of the office, I walked into the waiting room and saw this same young woman sitting there with her mother. My first thought was, oh no, what's gone wrong? But nothing had gone wrong. They had just come in to give me a gift. The mother said, "At this time of the year we just want to be thankful. So we want to thank you for returning her to health."

I found that very impactful. That was a very nice thing.

Addicted to Technology

Shimi Kang

Photo by Sham Sharma

A COUPLE OF GENERATIONS AGO, parents worried about their kids watching too much TV. They'd shoo them out of the house and that would solve the problem, at least for that day. Today television may be the least of a parent's worries. Technology doesn't sit in the corner of the living room; it sits in our pockets. Especially for young people, the desire to be digitally connected—to spend hour after hour on electronic devices—can become all-consuming.

Shimi Kang is a Vancouver psychiatrist who specializes in adolescent addiction. She has written books and makes regular media appearances to try to help people deal with tech addiction.

The human brain doesn't finish maturing until about age twenty-five, so I see technology addiction in many young people and slightly older people. In fact, internet addiction disorder has become a medical diagnosis, and any pediatrician or family doctor will tell you it is a huge issue—one of the biggest health issues of our time.

Just last week I saw a parent try to take a phone away from her fourteen-year-old daughter. The girl attacked her parent in front of everybody. This is an otherwise normal girl—a sweet kid who plays soccer and does other normal teenage things—but she was on her phone too much. Unable to tolerate it anymore, her mother took the phone away—and her daughter physically attacked her. I hear these stories all the time. All the time. Parents say, "I don't know what's going on with my kid and I don't know what to do."

A few years ago, I was invited to speak at an event in Chicago. There was a series of people speaking, so I only had about forty-five minutes. I was in an auditorium facing a mixed group of about four hundred parents, young people and teachers. The general topic was how to raise healthy, happy, self-motivated people, and I wanted to say something that would have lasting impact in their classrooms, schools and homes. I knew they were all interested in the effects of technology, and I knew I would get questions about it. Is it good or bad? Does it lead to anxiety, depression or addiction? Although everyone is worried about how technology is affecting the developing brain, we recognize its profound ability to take us further than we could ever have imagined. It's also a great equalizer in education, helping children with learning issues and accessibility. We need to talk about all of this, but there's a lot of confusion about how to start the conversation. How do we teach our children and each other about this powerful thing we call technology?

The answers aren't easy, and frankly I wasn't satisfied with some of the answers I had given on these issues in the past. I was trying to think of something quick that would satisfy this big crowd. I started by giving my usual talk, which included telling them about neuroscience and the things that I'd learned and used in my practice as a doctor for almost twenty years. I explained how technology impacts the human brain. Then I said, "Let's look at an analogy with something else that we do. We teach our children about diet. We teach them about food, and we start when they're very young—when they're babies. We tell them what's a treat, what's junk food and what's healthy food. We guide them along this path. Well, just like the food we eat impacts our bodies, the technology we consume impacts our minds."

I laid out this diet metaphor on the spot. I hadn't really formulated it beforehand. I was just speaking directly to these individuals as people who have the tools but need some guidance about the science.

When I talked about a tech diet, I explained that tech has the same categories, and the way we can understand it is based on the chemicals that are underneath our consumption or experience of food versus technology. For example, an hour of Instagram could be toxic if we're comparing our own lives to someone else's and concluding that, oh, they're doing better than me. Thinking that way can trigger the release of cortisol and adrenalin, which are stress hormones. They lead to a reduction in our immune response, increased heart rate—all kinds of terrible things. That can happen with just one hour of Instagram.

So that's comparable to toxic food. It's toxic tech. Of course, online hate and cyber-bullying are also toxic, but using technology for long periods to determine you aren't keeping up with others in some way is the kind of toxicity that people don't instantly recognize. Some tech is a little better, but we still have to be careful with it. Foods like chips and cookies give us a little hit of dopamine. That's a hormone that makes us feel good, but it's also associated with binge-eating. Even if we don't become addicted to eating, we might sometimes mindlessly eat a whole bag of chips or candy, which is not good.

That's what happens with this type of technology consumption, too. We might be mindlessly surfing Twitter, Facebook, Instagram or even a news feed, which is okay in limited amounts. But as we consume more and more junk tech, it starts to impact our health because it can lead to a sedentary lifestyle. If I'm crouched over a computer and I'm multitasking and not focused, my neurons are asking: Why are you crouched over in that posture? Why can't you concentrate? Is there a hurricane outside? Is that why you stay in this cave? Why are you not moving? In other words, we're sending a lot of stress signals to our neurosystem, which is releasing stress hormones—and we don't even realize it.

Finally, there are healthy snacks, which really comes down to endorphins. These are chemicals that interact with the receptors in your brain to trigger a positive feeling in the body. For example, I can use technology, like a walking app, to make myself healthier. I can slap headphones on and listen to music when I go for a run. Lots of people use technology to facilitate cardiovascular exercise.

Healthy technology can also facilitate a human connection. We can use Skype or FaceTime to call a friend or our grandmother, which elevates the oxytocin level in the body. It's the so-called "love hormone" because it increases empathy, trust and relationship building. All good. Some technology might help us to express ourselves creatively, releasing serotonin, the "happy chemical," which contributes to well-being and happiness.

This framework for understanding the effects of technology on health is based in science. It shows how our bodies use five or six neurochemicals, which may not be part of most people's daily vocabulary, by comparing that with food and eating and diet, which we're all accustomed to. It makes sense of a very big topic that people often find frustrating and overwhelming. When I first used this framework that time in Chicago, it was as if I'd turned on a light for the people in that auditorium. They got it. They had a deeper understanding and a bit more hope. It gave them a way to speak with their kids, their students, their community, their spouses, their boyfriends.

I started using that analogy a lot. I wrote about it, too. I created a webinar around it, which was posted, and we donated the money we made to Common Sense Media, a not-for-profit organization dedicated to helping kids in a world of media and technology. BBC News picked it up and interviewed me about the tech diet solution—and that interview got translated into about twenty languages. So as the message has spread, it has had a greater impact. It allows people to help themselves and others.

When I reflect on it all, I say, "Wow, this is what I want to be doing! This is what it means to be a physician, to take really solid science and an understanding that may not be accessible to the average person and deliver it in a way that is very accessible and very practical. To really empower people to make better choices." That's when I really feel great about what I do.

Stopping a Killer

David Sachar

Photo credit: Icahn School of Medicine at Mount Sinai

IT'S NOT OFTEN THAT A DOCTOR CAN SAY he had a hand in saving more than fifty million lives. David Sachar can.

Fifty years ago, cholera was a killer that could be treated only with intense methods in a well-equipped hospital, and in most of the world, that just wasn't happening. Millions of people were dying every year. Dr. Sachar was part of a small team that came up with a way to treat people much more easily and quickly. It's called "oral rehydration therapy." The prestigious *Lancet* medical journal, says it is "potentially the most important medical advance" of the twentieth century. The United Nations says no other medical innovation of the century "has had the potential to prevent so many deaths over such a short period of time and at so little cost."

David Sachar is a gastroenterologist. He is clinical professor of medicine and director emeritus of the GI division of Mount Sinai Medical Center in New York.

I n 1963 I still thought of myself as a medical student—though I was, in fact, a newly minted doctor. John F. Kennedy was president and the Peace Corps had just emerged with the idea that, as young Americans, we could change the world.

The speaker for our class day, which was essentially our graduation day at Harvard, was the Nobel Prize-winning parasitologist Thomas Weller, and he pointed out to us that the money the US government was spending on health research was at least ten times more than was being spent on international health. Even if everything we were doing for cancer, heart disease and stroke were successful, he said, that would only advance the life expectancy of Americans from 68.1 years to 69.5 years, or something like that. But if that same amount of money were spent on health concerns in the developing world, life expectancy there would go from say forty to sixty years. Very impressive.

Back then, we graduates all had a government obligation of a couple of years after school, and many of my classmates at the Harvard Medical School thought it would be really dandy to serve their time at the National Institutes of Health or the Bethesda Naval Hospital or the Walter Reed Army Medical Center. But I was all fired up to go somewhere to save the world, somewhere in the developing world. I went to my chief of medicine and I told him what I wanted, and he said, "I happen to know the guy who is the clinical director of the National Institutes of Health, and he's now in East Pakistan [now Bangladesh] helping to found a cholera research laboratory. It's being set up under the auspices of the US Agency for International Development, the State Department, the National Institutes of Health and the Southeast Asia Treaty Organization, SEATO."

I said, "That's where I want to go."

It was everything. It was a prestigious assignment. It was the National Institutes of Health. I would be a commissioned officer in the US Public Health Service, and it bore rather directly on the field of gastroenterology, which was an emerging specialty interest of mine. So I said, "That's perfect."

I went through some interviews and got the assignment. My colleagues were very supportive—in a sarcastic way. They said, "You're going to a cholera hospital. That's terrific! When you come back, you can treat all the cholera cases in Boston." It was a typical kind of Harvard doctor snobbish attitude. If it doesn't exist in Boston, it doesn't exist. So who cares? Meanwhile, it was killing two million people a year. But I was excited and off I went to East Pakistan with my wife and ten-month-old baby.

Cholera kills people by sucking all the fluid out of their bodies. They die in a couple of hours. At the time, the theory on choleric diarrhea was that somehow the cholera organism or its toxin poisoned the sodium pump, the mechanism by which sodium (salt) and thereby water is reabsorbed from the intestinal tract. Bob Gordon, the clinical director of the laboratory, had a brilliant insight. We already knew there is an electrical charge of a few millivolts across the wall of the intestine, created by the way sodium moves across the membrane. So, if the cholera organism was paralyzing the sodium pump and no sodium was moving, it should change the electrical charge across the wall of the intestine. So Bob said, "Why don't you figure out a way to measure the electricity inside the intestine?" If we could do that, we'd know whether the theory on what was causing cholera to kill people was correct.

Then Naval Captain Robert A. Phillips, the newly appointed director of the lab, said, "I happen to know someone in the field of medical electro physiology—Hans Ussing." Hans had a lab in Copenhagen where he had developed something called the Ussing

Chamber. It was a place where you could do experiments with a frog skin that had the ability to pump sodium, and you could measure the effect of various chemicals.

I went to Copenhagen for a couple of months and saw how the system worked, and from that we figured out a way to measure the electrical charge in the intestine of a living human. Then I went back to Dhaka and we got ready. The device we used was a pH meter, which would measure the electrical charge in the intestine. We would do it by having the patient swallow a tube so it would go down into the intestine. Then we would put another tube on the skin of the forearm. By measuring the electrical current between these two, we thought we might be able to measure the electrical charge across the intestinal wall.

While this was developing, I was rummaging through the old books and journals in the laboratory library, and I came across an article that described measuring the electrical potential in an animal. It pointed out that adding sugar to the lining inside the intestine would boost the electrical potential. I thought, here's a good way to see if our system is valid. So, we had a patient swallow the tube and we dripped a neutral solution into the intestine. Then we switched the solution from an ordinary salt drip to one containing glucose. I was sitting there at the machine, watching the needle that was measuring the electricity, when the needle went off the dial. That was the moment we realized it was possible to measure the sodium transport activity in a human being, not only in a normal state, but right at the height of cholera. It was the moment we realized the theory of what caused people to die from cholera was wrong. We could see the sodium pump wasn't paralyzed. We could see that adding sugar stimulated the electrical charge. There was actually a huge increase in electrical activity.

We were very excited, very pleased. The technician and I were dancing around the laboratory. We proved we had a good system.

Then in came Norbert Hirschhorn, the director of clinical research at the lab, and he asked, "What are you so excited about?"

I said, "The system works! We put in the glucose and the electric potential went up just the way it's supposed to."

He said, "That's terrific! That proves that if we add glucose, we'll boost the sodium pump, and we can treat patients that way."

In fact, this was an idea that Dr. Phillips had come up with some years before, but when he'd tried to treat patients in the Philippines, the experiment had gone badly. The concentration of ingredients in his solution wasn't right, and some little kids had died. So now Phillips didn't want anything to do with this kind of treatment.

But Dr. Hirschhorn thought the treatment was a great idea. Of course, I'm a scientist so I said, "Bert, you're getting way ahead of yourself to use this as therapy. This is still in the laboratory phase. It's an experiment. We are just showing that the theory works."

He said, "No, no, no. I think we should really use it as therapy," and he went to Dr. Phillips.

Having been burned once, Phillips said, "There's no way you are doing it. I don't want to go through that again." Bert persisted and finally Phillips reluctantly agreed—but only, he said, "if you have a doctor in the room with the patient twenty-four hours a day monitoring his condition."

That's how we ended up doing scientific experiments with live patients who were actually suffering from the effects of cholera. Bert Hirschhorn and I and others took turns sleeping with patients at the height of their cholera. We were dripping a glucose and salt solution down into their intestines, and sure enough it was working. The patients were getting better, which showed definitively that the conventional wisdom was wrong. The sodium pump was not paralyzed during cholera. It was, in fact, able to respond robustly to the addition of glucose just as a normal intestine would. The clinical experiment proved our theory was right. The glucose stimulated the electric potential in the intestine, and that was a dramatically effective treatment of the disease.

When we published our findings, it made a big splash. People were really excited by this.

Patients came into our hospital in Dhaka virtually dead. They had no palpable pulse, no blood pressure. They could maybe take two breaths a minute, and the blood in their bodies was fatally acidic. We would get an IV into them, start pouring the fluid into them, and within thirty minutes or an hour they'd be sitting up and eating and then walking around. It was just the fluids being sucked out of their bodies that was killing them. Once we got the fluids back in, they were fine. There was nothing else wrong with them.

The following year other investigators tried out our method at a field hospital in a rural village where they didn't have sophisticated equipment, and it worked there. Then they took it out to other rural villages and taught the process to mothers, and it worked there. The breakthrough was in the method of getting the fluids into the patients without taking them hundreds of miles to a hospital that had sterile intravenous bottles and fluids and needles. By the time they do that, the patient is most likely dead. But if, as soon as the cholera hits, the mothers in the field have this solution—these little packets of oral rehydration salts—they can put it in water or coconut juice and feed it to the kids, and the kids live.

And it's not just for cholera. Cholera is the super villain, but diarrheal disease is the number one cause of infant mortality in the world.

People still die of cholera. In some cases they're just too far gone to save. If the infection is too strong and the person is malnourished or deficient in vitamins or proteins or has parasites to begin with and lives in poverty and they get hit too hard and it takes too long to get treatment, they will still die. But the fatality rate has been cut dramatically.

This story is the best example I know of how you go from basic science in a laboratory to a hospital bedside to a field hospital to the most remote villages in just a couple of years. And to go from seemingly abstract basic scientific research to something that has literally saved a couple of million lives a year, that's gratifying. And I'm proud of it. It is certainly part of why I'm thrilled that I'm a doctor.

The Worst Day
of Somebody
Else's Life

Jeffrey Eppler

NOBODY WAKES UP IN THE MORNING AND thinks, I sure hope I have to go the hospital emergency department today. It's the last place we want to spend time because it can become, quite literally, the last place we ever spend time.

Jeffrey Eppler practises emergency medicine at Kelowna General Hospital. He loves his job, blending skill and knowledge with compassion and a certain toughness, too.

I remember a few years back I was giving a lecture to a group of paramedics. At the end of the talk I said to them, "Remember, the most important thing we can give a patient is early defibrillation."

One paramedic held up his hand and said, "Jeff, the most important thing we can give a patient is a warm blanket."

It was a profound moment in my life. It's so easy to get caught up in technology and cutting-edge practice, but at the end of the day it's kindness that a patient needs. I thought: He's so right. It doesn't matter how smart you are or if you know the latest paper in the *New England Journal of Medicine*. If you're not holding somebody's hand and being really kind to them, if you're not demonstrating compassion, it doesn't really mean a lot to patients. That was a turning point for me.

I remember early on in my residency I had begun to wonder if all the extra training I was doing to become an emergency doctor was worth the trouble. It was a five-year program after medical school. I was having a very busy day in Emergency. I was on my way to the bathroom, but they called for a doctor in resuscitation, so I turned around and went back to see this patient.

It was a young man in cardiac arrest. The team was doing CPR on him. I looked at the monitor, which showed his heart was in a rhythm called "ventricular tachycardia." The heart is beating so fast that it doesn't pump efficiently so it's not delivering much blood to the brain and the body. In many cases that is not compatible with life. This case was kind of weird because it's usually older people who are in ventricular tachycardia. Young people can get it too, but it's much rarer. I said, "Put the paddles on him." We defibrillated him but nothing much happened. He wasn't responding at all.

I said to myself, this doesn't make any sense.

Then he started to have a seizure, and that's when one of the paramedics said, "He's some kind of schizo or something." It's a terrible term for sure, but at that moment the penny dropped. I thought: Oh my god, this guy is not in cardiac crisis. He's taken an overdose of antidepressants!

I told the nurses, "Quick, give him sodium bicarbonate." That's the antidote for an antidepressant overdose, and I watched as his heart went back to a normal rhythm. Afterwards he was taken to the intensive care unit and he recovered fully.

At that moment it all crystallized for me. I thought: I'm doing all this extra training for a good reason. Because of my training I was able to intervene and save this guy's life. I know things other people don't know. A lot of people would have missed the diagnosis. I now have an expertise in emergency medicine and it's paid off. It's all worth it.

That was an amazing moment, and I've had many more in the years since then. I've come to realize that suffering is universal, so every day I try to reduce people's suffering. The thing about emergency medicine is that you see whoever comes through the door. You don't turn anybody away. That's what I love most about the job. I love the fact that you help everybody no matter where they come from. They can be the most nasty-smelling, homeless person or someone rich and famous or somebody in between. You never know what the day is going to throw at you. It could be a gunshot wound. It could be a confused elderly person with pneumonia. It could be a little kid with a seizure. You take care of everyone. You show kindness to everyone. And you don't judge anyone.

I don't believe we should be locking people up if they want to get high. I'm a great believer in harm reduction. As long as a person isn't hurting anybody else or driving a car, I don't judge them if they take drugs. That's why I volunteer at music festivals.

I was working at one last year and it was crazy. There were people coming into the medical area high on LSD, high on mushrooms. One guy who came in was really, really, really messed up. He had done three doses of MDMA—what most of the world calls "ecstasy." It's a party drug we see a lot at music festivals. He was extremely agitated. His eyes were going in every direction. His pupils were as big as saucers. He wasn't quite in seizure, but he was exhibiting this crazy movement where his muscles were stiffening up. His mind was completely altered, and he was unintelligible. When I talked to him, he couldn't understand me, and he couldn't follow commands. He was also extremely hyperthermic—that is, his body temperature was way up. Ecstasy can cause your body to overheat, which cooks your brains. It can leave you with permanent brain damage or it can kill you.

Because of my training in poisoning and toxicology, I knew this guy was at risk, but luckily I had prepared for this in advance. I had asked the music festival to build me a cryobath, which is basically a wooden box that we lined with plastic and filled with ice water. We were already giving the patient muscle relaxants. I said, "We have to throw him in the ice bath." So we threw him in, and his temperature went from 39° to 37°, which is normal. The horrible seizure-like movements stopped. Within twenty minutes to a half-hour he was awake and talking to me, completely rational. If I hadn't had training and expertise, that guy probably would have died.

Before I sent him on his way, I said, "You can't do more drugs tonight."

And he said, "I can't promise you that, Doc."

I said, "Okay. We're here if you need us."

That's a lot of what we do in emergency medicine. We take care of people no matter what. Sometimes we take care of them because of the results of their bad decisions. It can be too much alcohol or cigarettes, not enough good eating or exercise or choosing to do one more ski run when they're already tired. Whatever. People make bad decisions all the time. My job is to never judge them for their bad decisions but try to keep them out of harm's way and educate them.

I deal with addictions on a daily basis, but in the last two or three years I have treated way more opioid overdoses than I treated in the previous twenty. I treated a guy last year who took an overdose of opioids. We brought him around and I kept him overnight because he was pretty drowsy. When it was safe for him to leave, I tried to link him up with resources to help him. I said, "Be careful. It's dangerous out there. If you don't take care, you're going to die." He fatally overdosed the next day.

So what are you going do with that? Here's a guy I had talked to, told him I wanted to help him, tried to push him in the right direction. And then I found out the next day that he'd died. It's horrible, and it makes me sad. The only sense I can make of that is to show how potent a disease addiction is. But I have to carry on. I have to have a little bit of a shell. I care about people, but I can't let that kind of stuff get under my skin. If I did, I couldn't do my job.

I've seen horrible things over the years. But then I walk out of the trauma room and there are nine or ten patients waiting to be seen, and they all legitimately need help. They have chest pain, intestinal bleeding, strokes, pneumonia. I can't indulge myself. I have to dust myself off and move on. It's not insensitivity or a lack of empathy. I owe it to the other patients to keep moving. Sometimes the things that happen really bother me, but I can't let them get to me because then I can't function and take care of other people.

I have never worked a day where I haven't felt I've made a big difference in somebody's life. We go into medicine because we want to help people. I want to be careful as I say this, and maybe it's hard to understand if you're not in the profession, but very often the most rewarding day you have is the worst day of somebody else's life. If I step in and bring someone back from the brink of death, that patient has been through hell, but I've had a gratifying day. It's a terrible paradox.

Every day in my job I get to help people out. I take away their pain. I take away their worry. I do something positive for them. That's a great gift and a great blessing for me. I'm not better than the guy who does an honest day's work on an assembly line. I just happen to be in a position where I can have an immediate impact on people. I view that as a privilege, and I never take it for granted. I really believe that in my heart.

About the Author

Mark Bulgutch

Photo courtesy Gary Gould

MARK BULGUTCH WORKED FOR CBC News for over thirty-five years. He is the recipient of fourteen Gemini awards, four Radio Television News Directors Association awards, the Canadian Journalism Foundation Award of Excellence and the Canadian Association of Broadcasters Gold Ribbon Award. His previous book, *That's Why I'm a Journalist* (Douglas & McIntyre), was released in 2015. He currently lives in Toronto, ON.